Marine Chartwork

Marine Chartwork

SECOND EDITION

D A Moore

ADLARD COLES NAUTICAL
London

Published by Adlard Coles Nautical
an imprint of A & C Black (Publishers) Ltd
35 Bedford Row, London WC1R 4JH

© D A Moore 1967, 1981

First edition 1967
Published as *Marine Chartwork and Navaids*
Reprinted 1970, 1973, 1975
Second edition 1981
Reprinted 1982, 1984, 1988, 1991

ISBN 0 7136 3438 3

A CIP catalogue record for this book is available from
the British Library.

Printed in Great Britain by
J W Arrowsmith Ltd, Bristol

PREFACE

The history of navigation extends from the earliest use of landmarks to the modern techniques of electronic navigation and embraces a science with many and varied facets.

The purpose of this book is to present the underlying principles of the technique of sailing coastwise to students for the RYA/D.Tp. and GCE examinations, where the respective syllabuses are more than adequately covered. it will prove invaluable to yachtsmen who wish to venture beyond their home estuary.

The principles involved in finding and plotting position lines are thoroughly explained with many worked examples. The basic navigational principles are simply explained and the text is well illustrated with diagrams throughout.

I am indebted to the Controller of H.M. Stationery Office and the Hydrographer of the Navy for permission to produce sections of various charts and tidal publications. My thanks are also due to those who have given so much of their time in assisting with the preparation of this book and in the tedious work of checking and proof reading. Whilst every effort has been made to ensure accuracy I would be pleased to hear of any errors that may have occurred.

D A Moore

CONTENTS

DEFINITIONS

The following terms standardised by the Nautical Institute have been accepted by the Dept of Transport and the Royal Navy and adopted by the RYA for the teaching and examination of yachtsmen.

TRACK   The path followed or to be followed between one position and another. This path may be that **over the ground** (ground track) or **through the water** (water track).

GROUND TRACK   Course made good over the ground.

WATER TRACK   Course allowing for leeway.

TRACK ANGLE   The direction of a track (in degrees).

HEADING   The horizontal direction of the ship's head at a given moment. (This term does not necessarily require movement of the vessel.)

COURSE (Co)   The intended heading.

COURSE TO STEER   The course related to the compass used by the helmsman.

SET   The direction towards which a current and/or tidal stream flows.

DRIFT   The distance covered in a given time due solely to the movement of a current and/or tidal stream.

DRIFT or DRIFT ANGLE   The angular difference (degrees) between the ground track and water track.

LEEWAY   The effect of wind in moving a vessel bodily to leeward.

LEEWAY ANGLE   The angular difference (degrees) between the water track and the ship's heading.

SEA POSITION   The point at the termination of the water track.

DEAD RECKONING   Maintaining or predicting an approximate record of progress by projecting course and distance from a known position (symbol +).

DR POSITION   A position obtained by dead reckoning, i.e. using True course and distance run, the latter derived from the log or engine revolutions.

ESTIMATED POSITION (EP)   A best possible approximation of a present or future position, based on course and distance since the last known position with an estimation made for leeway, set and drift; or by extrapolation from previous position fixes.

Finding an Estimated Position

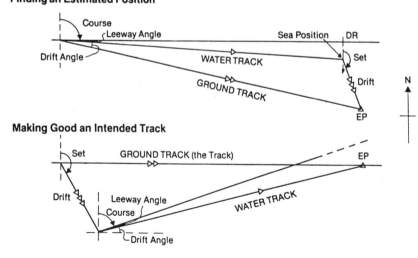

Making Good an Intended Track

1
DIRECTION AND CO-ORDINATES

THE EARTH has three components in its movement in space. The first, which is not detectable, is the general translation of the Solar System through space. The remaining two, which are detectable, are:

1. A yearly passage in an elliptical path about the Sun.
2. A daily rotation about a fixed axis.

It is the latter that gives rise to the four cardinal directions.

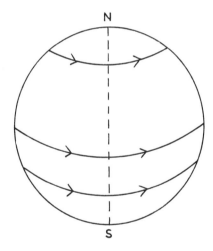

In the figure, NS is the fixed axis about which the Earth rotates once each day and the points N and S where this diameter meets the surface are known as the poles.

East is the direction in which any point on the Earth's surface is being carried by the rotation and is shown by the arrows.

West is the direction 180° from East.

North is the direction lying 90° to the left of an observer facing east, the pole lying in this direction is referred to as the north pole.

South and the south pole lie 90° to the right of the same observer.

Having obtained the four cardinal directions, the angle between each of these is sub-divided into eight parts known as points each having an angular measure of $11\frac{1}{4}°$. They are named from the two adjacent cardinal points. The point is then further sub-divided into four equal parts known as quarter points.

1

Points				Angular Measure
North	East	South	West	0°
N by E	E by S	S by W	W by N	11° 15'
NNE	ESE	SSW	WNW	22° 30'
NE by N	SE by E	SW by S	NW by W	33° 45'
NE	SE	SW	NW	45° 00'
NE by E	SE by S	SW by W	NW by N	56° 15'
ENE	SSE	WSW	NNW	67° 30'
E by N	S by E	W by S	N by W	78° 45'
East	South	West	North	90° 00'

The use of points is confined these days, in general, to indicate wind direction, but even this is falling into disuse. The modern method of indicating direction is to use the 360° notation, i.e. North is 000° or 360°, all other directions being measured clockwise from North.

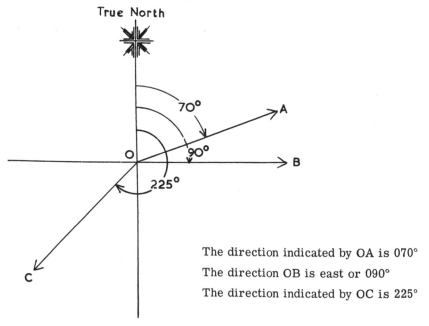

The direction indicated by OA is 070°

The direction OB is east or 090°

The direction indicated by OC is 225°

The navigator at sea has no indication of direction by merely surveying the horizon. The instrument he uses is the ship's compass.

Most modern ships are fitted with a gyro-compass which takes its reference from true north or the true geographical meridian, hence the course steered is the angle made by the ship's head with true geographic north and is known as the <u>true course</u>.

The magnetic compass, still a compulsory but often neglected piece of equipment on merchant ships, uses the magnetic meridian as its reference. Unfortunately the magnetic and geographic poles are not coincident and consequently there will always be some angle between the true and magnetic meridians (except when the true and magnetic poles are in the same line).

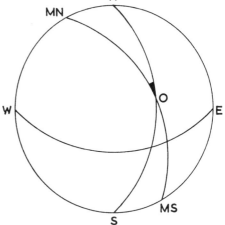

In the figure, N and S represent the geographic north and south poles respectively. MN and MS represent the magnetic north and south poles. Angle N O MN is the angle between the true and magnetic meridians at O.

This angle between the two meridians is known as variation (sometimes referred to as declination among non-seafarers) and is named east when magnetic north is to the right of true north, and west when magnetic north is to the left of true north. The angle that the ship's head makes with the magnetic meridian is known as the <u>magnetic course</u>.

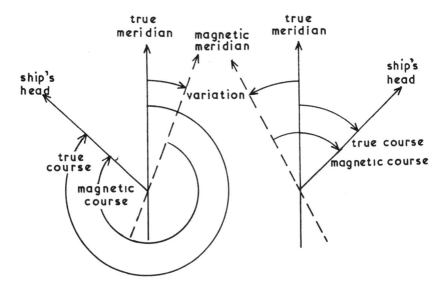

From the diagram it can be seen that to convert magnetic courses to true, the variation is added when east and subtracted when west.

A further complication arises with the use of magnetic compasses on board ship, the steel structure invariably has some residual magnetic effect. The net result is to deflect the magnetic needle away from the magnetic meridian to a greater or lesser degree dependent upon the ship's head. This deflection is known as deviation and is named east when the deflection is to the right of the magnetic meridian and west when the deflection is to the left. The course indicated by a magnetic compass influenced by both variation and deviation is known as the compass course.

The combination of variation and deviation is known as the error of the magnetic compass.

TO OBTAIN THE AMOUNT AND NAME OF THE ERROR
Variation and deviation same names - add - error has the same name.
Variation and deviation different names - take the difference - error takes the name of the greater.

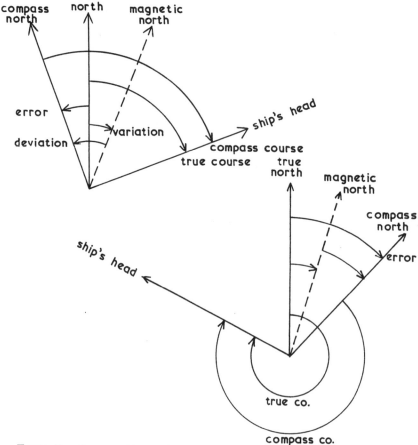

From the diagram it can be seen that to obtain the true course the error must be added to the compass course when east and subtracted when west. The reverse applies when converting true headings to compass.

One other aspect of direction must be considered and that is the direction of one object from an observer or from another object, this direction is termed the bearing.

True bearing is the angle between the direction of the place or object in question and the direction of true north.

Magnetic bearing is the angle between the direction of the place or object and the magnetic meridian.

Compass bearing is the angle between the direction of the place or object and the direction of compass north.

NOTE. The navigator must bear in mind that when using a compass on board ship, the bearing obtained is a compass bearing and must be corrected for the compass error to obtain the true bearing.

It is usual to append the suffixes C. M. and T. to bearings and courses to indicate compass, magnetic and true, respectively.

Worked Example

Ships's head by compass 033°. Deviation 5°E. Variation 10°E. Find the compass error and the true and magnetic courses.

Compass course	033°		
Deviation	5°E		
Magnetic course	038°	Variation	10°E
Variation	10°E	Deviation	5°E
True course	048°	Error	15°E

Worked Example

Ship's head by compass 327°. Error 16°W. Find the true course and, if the variation is 20°W., find and name the deviation.

Compass course	327°	Error	16°W
Error	16°W	Variation	20°W
True course	311°	Deviation	4°E

Worked Example

The compass bearing of a distant object was 006°. The true bearing was known to be 349°. Find the error of the compass.

True bearing	349°	
Compass bearing	366°	(360° added for convenience)
Error	17°W	

Compasses are adjusted by means of magnetic correctors to reduce the deviations so that the compass will be steadier and give a more positive indication of amount of turn. The residual deviations are tabulated by the compass adjuster for the navigator's reference. The tabulation may be translated into a simple curve and the deviation for any compass heading read directly. However, to find the deviation to make good a given magnetic course would require the superimposition of a second curve giving the deviations for magnetic headings.

The tabulation shown below gives rather large values of deviations and it is possible that these would not be tolerated on board ship, they are given here for the purpose of illustrating typical problems that arise.

DEVIATION TABLE A

Ship's head by compass	Deviation	Ship's head by compass	Deviation
North	10° W	South	10° E
N by E	4° W	S by W	$11\frac{1}{2}$° E
NNE	$1\frac{1}{2}$° E	SSW	$12\frac{1}{2}$° E
NE by N	$6\frac{1}{2}$° E	SW by S	12° E
NE	10° E	SW	10° E
NE by E	12° E	SW by W	$6\frac{1}{2}$° E
ENE	$12\frac{1}{2}$° E	WSW	$1\frac{1}{2}$° E
E by N	$11\frac{1}{2}$° E	W by S	4° W
East	10° E	West	10° W
E by S	8° E	W by N	$15\frac{1}{2}$° W
ESE	6° E	WNW	20° W
SE by E	$4\frac{1}{2}$° E	NW by W	23° W
SE	4° E	NW	24° W
SE by S	$4\frac{1}{2}$° E	NW by N	23° W
SSE	6° E	NNW	20° W
S by E	8° E	N by W	$15\frac{1}{2}$° W
South	10° E	North	10° W

DEVIATION TABLE B

Ship's head by compass	Deviation	Ship's head by compass	Deviation
000°	10° W	180°	10° E
010°	$4\frac{1}{2}$° W	190°	$11\frac{1}{2}$° E
020°	$\frac{1}{2}$° E	200°	$12\frac{1}{2}$° E
030°	5° E	210°	$12\frac{1}{2}$° E
040°	$8\frac{1}{2}$° E	220°	11° E
050°	11° E	230°	$8\frac{1}{2}$° E
060°	$12\frac{1}{2}$° E	240°	5° E
070°	$12\frac{1}{2}$° E	250°	$\frac{1}{2}$° E
080°	$11\frac{1}{2}$° E	260°	$4\frac{1}{2}$° W
090°	10° E	270°	10° W
100°	8° E	280°	15° W
110°	$6\frac{1}{2}$° E	290°	19° W
120°	5° E	300°	$22\frac{1}{2}$° W
130°	$4\frac{1}{2}$° E	310°	24° W
140°	$4\frac{1}{2}$° E	320°	24° W
150°	5° E	330°	$22\frac{1}{2}$° W
160°	$6\frac{1}{2}$° E	340°	19° W
170°	8° E	350°	15° W
180°	10° E	360°	10° W

DEVIATION CURVE

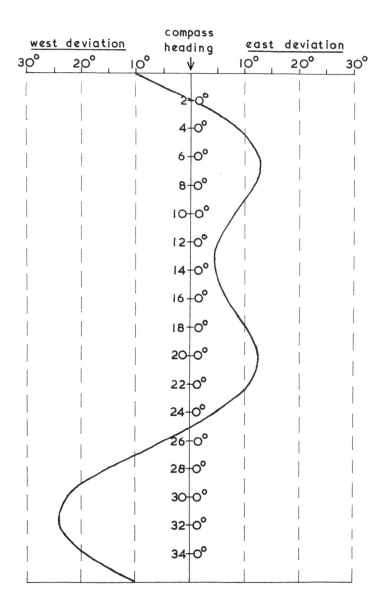

west deviation   compass heading   east deviation

TO FIND THE DEVIATION FOR A GIVEN COMPASS COURSE

This is a simple matter of direct interpolation between the deviations for the two adjacent headings on either side of the required course.

Worked Example

What is the deviation for a compass course of 336° ?

From Table A

NW by N or	$326\frac{1}{4}°$ C	dev.	23° W	$326\frac{1}{4}°$
NNW or	$337\frac{1}{2}°$ C	dev.	20° W	336°
differences	$11\frac{1}{4}°$		3°	$9\frac{3}{4}°$

for a heading change of $11\frac{1}{4}°$ the deviation changes 3°

for a heading change of 1° the deviation changes $\dfrac{3°}{11\frac{1}{4}°}$

therefore for a heading change of $9\frac{3}{4}°$ the deviation will change:-

$$\frac{3}{11\frac{1}{4}} \times 9\frac{3}{4}° = \frac{3}{1} \times \frac{4}{45} \times \frac{39}{4} = 2.6°$$

Deviation on 336° C = 23.0° W - 2.6° = <u>20.4° W</u>

From Table B

	330° C	dev.	$22\frac{1}{2}°$ W	330° C
	340° C	dev.	19° W	336° C
differences	10°		$3\frac{1}{2}°$	6°

for a heading change of 10° the deviation changes $3\frac{1}{2}°$

for a heading change of 1° the deviation changes $\dfrac{3\frac{1}{2}°}{10°}$

therefore for a heading change of 6° the deviation will change:-

$$\frac{3\frac{1}{2}}{10} \times 6° = \frac{7}{2} \times \frac{6}{10} = 2.1°$$

Deviation on 336° C = 22.5° W – 2.1° = <u>20.4° W</u>

TO FIND THE DEVIATION FOR A GIVEN TRUE COURSE

First the variation for the given time and place must be applied to obtain the magnetic course. Then from the deviation table two compass headings are selected so that when the deviations are applied the resultant magnetic headings lie either side of the magnetic course in question. The deviation is then obtained by direct interpolation.

Worked Example

What deviation must be allowed to make a true course of 017° if the variation is 12°W?

$$\begin{array}{ll}\text{True course} & 017° \\ \text{Variation} & \underline{12°\,W} \\ \text{Magnetic course} & 029°\end{array}$$

From Table A

N by E or	$011\frac{1}{4}°$ C	NNE or	$022\frac{1}{2}°$ C	NE by N or	$033\frac{3}{4}°$ C
deviations	$\underline{4°\ W}$		$\underline{1\frac{1}{2}°\,E}$		$\underline{6\frac{1}{2}°\,E}$
	$007\frac{1}{4}°$ M		$024°$ M		$040\frac{1}{4}°$ M

It is evident that the required deviation lies between $1\frac{1}{2}°$ E and $6\frac{1}{2}°$ E.

	024° M		024° M		dev. $1\frac{1}{2}°$ E
	029° M		$040\frac{1}{4}°$ M		dev. $6\frac{1}{2}°$ E
differences	5°		$16\frac{1}{4}°$		5°

for a heading change of $16\frac{1}{4}°$ the deviation changes $5°$

for a heading change of $1°$ the deviation changes $\dfrac{5°}{16\frac{1}{4}}$

therefore for a heading change of 5° the deviation will change:-

$$\frac{5}{16\frac{1}{4}} \times 5° = \frac{5 \times 4 \times 5}{65} = 1.5°$$

$$\text{deviation on 029° M} = 1.5°\,E + 1.5° = \underline{3.0°\,E}$$

From Table B

	010° C		020° C		030° C
deviations	$\underline{4\frac{1}{2}°\,W}$		$\underline{\frac{1}{2}°\,E}$		$\underline{5°\,E}$
	$005\frac{1}{2}°$ M		$020\frac{1}{2}°$ M		035° M

therefore the deviation for 029° M must lie between $\frac{1}{2}°$ E and 5° E.

	$020\frac{1}{2}°$ M		$020\frac{1}{2}°$ M		dev. $\frac{1}{2}°$ E
	029° M		035° M		dev. 5° E
differences	$8\frac{1}{2}°$		$14\frac{1}{2}°$		$4\frac{1}{2}°$

for a heading change of $14\frac{1}{2}°$ the deviation changes $4\frac{1}{2}°$

for a heading change of $1°$ the deviation changes $\dfrac{4\frac{1}{2}°}{14\frac{1}{2}°}$

therefore for a heading change of $8\frac{1}{2}°$ the deviation will change:-

$$\frac{4\frac{1}{2}}{14\frac{1}{2}} \times 8\frac{1}{2}° = \frac{9}{2} \times \frac{2}{29} \times \frac{17}{2} = 2.6°$$

$$\text{deviation on 029° M} = 0.5°\,E + 2.6° = \underline{3.1°\,E}$$

10

POSITION COORDINATES

It was previously stated that when a sphere is rotated it acquires a reference line, its spin axis. In the case of the earth this axis terminates in the north and south geographic poles. Midway between the poles a plane perpendicular to the spin axis intersects the surface of the earth in a line known as the Equator. All points on the Equator are equidistant from the poles and the plane of the Equator divides the earth into the Northern and Southern Hemispheres.

LATITUDE AND THE NAUTICAL MILE

Other planes can be passed through the earth which are all perpendicular to the spin axis and parallel to the Equator. These planes intersect the surface of the earth in lines known as parallels of latitude.

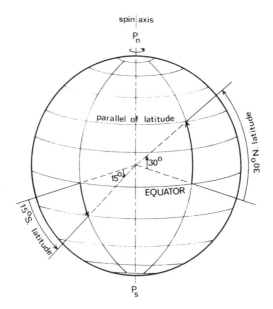

The figure illustrates the earth's spin axis, the geographic poles and parallels of latitude spaced at 15° intervals.

All points on the same parallel will have the same latitude which is named north (N) if the position is located in the Northern Hemisphere and south (S) if it is located in the Southern Hemisphere. However, because the earth is spheroidal in shape there are two types of latitude:
Geocentric latitude is defined as the angle measured from the centre of the earth north or south of the Equator.
Geographic latitude is defined as the angle between the normal to the spheroid and the plane of the Equator, i.e. it is measured from the centre of curvature of that place. It is geographic latitude that is used for surveying and navigational purposes.

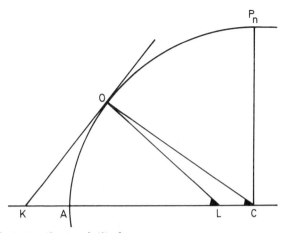

The figure illustrates the two latitudes.

0 is a point in the Northern Hemisphere
K0 is a tangent in a north/south direction to this point
L0 is the normal to this tangent intersecting CA at L
Angle 0LA is the geographic latitude of 0
Angle 0CA is the geocentric latitude of 0

It is evident that the difference between these latitudes will be zero at the poles and Equator and will have its maximum value when the geographic latitude is $45°$. This maximum value is approximately $11'.6$.

Geographic latitude also gives rise to a further definition, that of the <u>nautical mile</u> (M). This is defined as the length of the arc of a meridian subtending an arc of $1'.0$ at the centre of curvature of that place. Since the radius of curvature is minimum at the equator and maximum at the poles, the nautical mile will have <u>minimum</u> length at the <u>equator</u> and <u>maximum</u> length at the <u>poles.</u>

The Admiralty Manual of Navigation derives the formula for the nautical miles as:

$$(6077.1 - 30.7.\cos 2\phi) \text{ feet}$$

where ϕ is the geographic latitude.

The resultant length of the nautical mile is 6046.4 feet (1842.94 metres) at the equator and 6107.8 feet (1861.66 metres) at the poles.

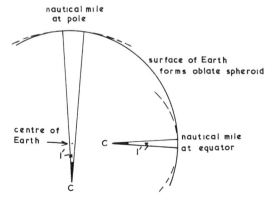

The International Nautical Mile has been established as 1852 metres (6076.12 feet) although in many countries a standard nautical mile of 6080 feet (1853.2 metres) is used. For purposes of standardisation the International Nautical Mile is used throughout this book.

The unit of speed used in navigation is the knot which is defined as a nautical mile per hour. In other words, a vessel moving at 15 knots is proceeding at 15 nautical miles per hour.

LONGITUDE

An infinite number of planes can be passed through the earth with the spin axis and both poles in the same plane. These planes intersect the surface of the earth in circles known as meridians. That half of a meridian extending from pole to pole on the same side of the earth as the observer is referred to as the upper branch and the half on the other side of the earth as the lower branch. All meridians will intersect the equator and the parallels of latitude at 90°. The reference meridian (0°) from which longitude is measured is the meridian of Greenwich, located in London, England and is often referred to as the prime meridian. Longitude is the angular measure east or west between the Greenwich meridian and the meridian passing through a given place.

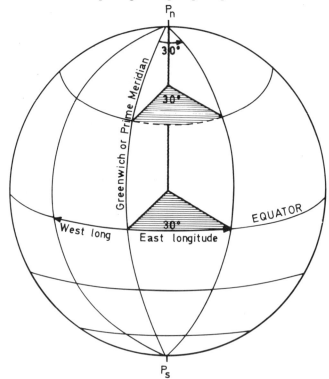

The figure illustrates that longitude may be measured:
  — along a parallel of latitude,
  — at the equator,
  — at the poles as the angle between the meridians as they converge.

It is evident that having established a series of reference lines (latitude and longitude) any position on the earth may be precisely located in these terms.

GREAT CIRCLES AND RHUMB LINES

A great circle is defined as any circle on a sphere whose plane divides the sphere into two equal parts. Examples of this are the meridians and the equator. An infinite number of great circles can be inscribed on a sphere and the section of such a circle passing between two points provides the shortest distance between these points. However, a great circle will intersect the meridians at different angles, the only exception being the equator. The navigator using his compass would be required to continuously change his course in order to accurately follow a great circle route. Since this would be impractical, it is customary to steer a constant course from point to point. This constant course line is known as a rhumb line or loxodromic curve. The rhumb line will cut all meridians through which it passes at the same angle: examples of this are parallels of latitude. The only time that a vessel can follow a rhumb line and also a great circle is on the equator or when steaming along a meridian.

On ocean passages when a great circle route may result in considerable saving in distance it is usual to plot several points along the great circle route and to steer rhumb lines between successive points.

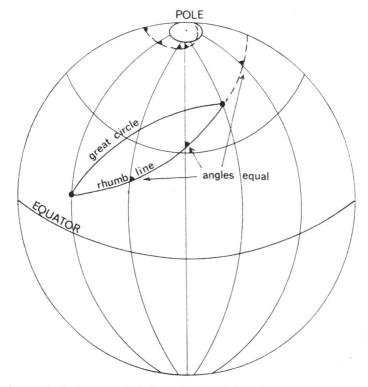

The figure illustrates a great circle and a rhumb line between two points on the surface of the earth. It should be noted that the rhumb line will spiral in toward the pole.

2
PROJECTIONS AND THE NAUTICAL CHART

It is quite evident that the surface of a sphere or spheroid such as the earth cannot be correctly represented on a plane, therefore any extensive portion of the surface so represented must involve distortion of some of the following qualities:

— shape
— bearing
— scale
— area

It is possible to derive a projection which will eliminate one or more of these distortions while keeping the others within acceptable limits.

MERCATOR PROJECTION

This is the most useful projection to the navigator. It allows him to draw a straight line from departure point to destination and to measure the steady course he has to maintain to arrive there.
    The projection is classed as a <u>cylindrical orthomorphic projection</u> in which:
1. rhumb lines appear as straight lines
2. the angles between rhumb lines are unaltered between chart and earth
3. the equator appears as a straight line
4. parallels of latitude appear as straight lines parallel to the equator
5. meridians appear as equally spaced parallel lines perpendicular to the equator
Because of this latter property the polar regions cannot be reproduced on this projection and it is rarely used beyond latitude 70° north or south.
    The projection preserves the shape of the land over small areas although distortion in area occurs. On a map of the world on a Mercator projection Greenland appears larger than South America although the latter is nearly nine times larger in area.
    The latitude scales are always on the left and right hand margins with north latitude increasing toward the top and south latitude increasing toward the bottom of the chart. The longitude scales are always on the upper and lower margins with west longitude increasing to the left and east longitude increasing to the right.

GNOMONIC PROJECTION

This is a true geometrical projection where the chart is drawn on a flat surface tangential to the Earth as shown in the diagram.

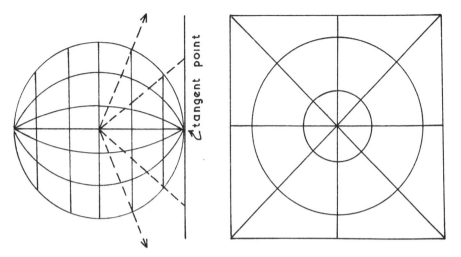

construction of a polar gnomonic chart

Straight lines are drawn from the centre of the Earth through points on the surface of the Earth thence to the chart. The result of this is that:
1. great circles appear as straight lines, hence the gnomonic chart is suitable for the plotting of great circle tracks;
2. meridians appear as straight lines converging at the poles;
3. rhumb lines appear as curves;
4. parallels of latitude appear as curves;
5. the greater the distance from the 'tangent point' the greater the distortion.

The gnomonic projection is used for polar charts, great circle sailing charts and charts having a natural scale greater than 1/50,000.

This projection is used principally by the navigator to plot great circle routes. The procedure being to transfer geographic points from the great circle route to the Mercator chart and to steer rhumb lines between each point.

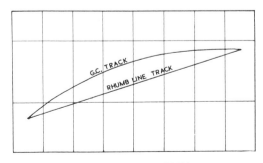

MERCATOR PROJECTION

16

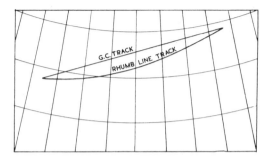

GNOMONIC PROJECTION

POLYCONIC PROJECTION

This is a conical projection but with each parallel of latitude being constructed as if it were the standard parallel of a simple conical projection, hence the term 'polyconic'. The parallels become arcs of circles, the radii of which steadily increase as the latitude decreases. The central meridian will appear as a straight line correctly divided, but the other meridians will no longer be straight lines. This projection is used for charts of the polar areas and by Canada and the United States for charts of the St. Lawrence Seaway and the Great Lakes. Its practical use will be explained in later chapters.

NAUTICAL CHARTS

A nautical chart is a representation of a portion of the earth's surface specifically designed for use in navigation. Unlike a map, it is intended to be worked upon, not merely looked at. It must readily permit the graphic solution of navigation problems such as direction and distance, or position determination in terms of latitude and longitude.

It contains information on coastlines, harbours, channels, obstructions, currents, depths of water and aids to navigation. The chart is probably the most important tool in the art of navigation and until the navigator can use it fully it will simply be a piece of paper.

Charts are divided into two main categories:
1. Navigational charts on which the ship's position and track can be plotted
2. Non-navigational charts that provide other information that is useful to the mariner, such as magnetic variation charts, current charts, route charts, ice charts, etc.

The former may be sub-divided into several secondary groups:
1. Ocean or Sailing charts on a very small scale depicting large areas
2. General charts of a larger scale for coastwise navigation
3. Coastal charts for inshore navigation
4. Harbour or Plan charts that are of the largest scale and give details of harbours, estuaries, canals and other small areas
5. Special charts issued by various governments such as the U.S. charts of the Intracostal Waterway and the Canadian charts of the St. Lawrence Seaway and the Great Lakes

Scale

The terms 'large' and 'small' scale often give rise to some confusion as to which is which. The natural scale of a map or chart is the ratio of a length measured on the chart to the corresponding length on the surface of the earth. It is expressed as a fraction.

The smaller the value of the fraction the smaller the scale. However, the term 'small' or 'large' in this case is relative. For example, a scale of 1/100,000 is smaller than a scale of 1/50,000 but it is larger than a scale of 1/200,000. A scale of 1/100,000 means that $1''$ on the chart corresponds to $100,000''$ on the surface of the earth, or $1''$ corresponds to 2,540 metres or 1.37 nautical miles.

The equator is shown on a Mercator chart as a straight line having some definite length, the longitude scale is therefore fixed by that length and will be constant in all latitudes. On the surface of the Earth however, the meridians converge towards the poles and consequently the Mercator chart distorts the Earth's surface in an east-west direction proportional to the distance from the equator. At the poles this distortion would be infinite, so that the projection cannot be used for polar regions. In order to preserve the correct shape of land masses (orthomorphy) the parallels of latitude are increasingly spaced towards the poles. This varying latitude scale, which governs distortion of distances in all directions, correctly indicates distances for all places in that latitude; therefore the scale of distance on any Mercator chart is the latitude scale provided that it is only used in that latitude.

In general, charts having a scale smaller than 1/50,000 are on the Mercator projection. Charts having a scale larger than 1/50,000 are on the polyconic projection, often erroneously referred to as the gnomonic projection. These charts are harbour charts and occasionally the longitude scale is omitted.

If a scale of longitude is not given on the plan it can be found from the construction shown:

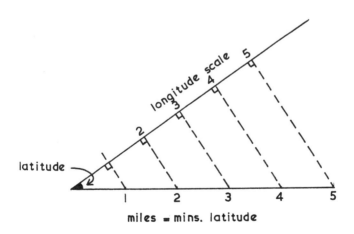

miles = mins. latitude

From the zero point of the distance or latitude scale construct a line making an angle equal to the latitude of the place. From each division of the distance scale construct a perpendicular to this line. The resultant scale is the longitude scale.

18

DESCRIPTION OF THE CHART

The navigator, particularly on vessels that are travelling worldwide, will meet a variety of charts published by the many maritime nations. It is not uncommon to find a mixture of charts including those published by both Government bodies and by commerical publishers.

The following remarks are of a general nature and some of the information given may not appear on all charts.

Number.   This is shown on the bottom right hand and upper left hand corners of the margin. It is the number of the chart from the catalogue of the issuing authority. The mariner may find, when consulting a catalogue that the prefix (L) appears before the number. This indicates that the appropriate chart has an overprint of either a Decca, Loran or Omega lattice.

Title or Legend   This is placed clear of the sea area and so that no essential navigational information is obscured.
Additional information usually given under the title includes:
a. the area depicted;
b. units of the soundings i.e. fathoms, feet or metres;
c. date of survey of the chart;
d. natural scale;
e. a reminder that all bearings given on the chart refer to the true meridian and are given from seaward.

Publication. This is shown in the middle of the lower margin.

Date of printing. This is shown in the right hand top corner outside the margin, e.g. 204.65 which means that the chart was printed on the 204th day of 1965.

Dimensions. These are shown in brackets at the bottom right corner. They denote the dimensions, in inches, of the chart between the inner lines of graduation. They are useful in providing a check if distortion is suspected.

Date of new editions. When a chart is thoroughly revised and modernised in style, a new edition is published and the date is shown to the right of the original date of publication. All large and small correction notations are erased and old copies of the chart should be replaced.

Large corrections. When a chart is corrected (not revised) from information too comprehensive to insert by hand, the date on which these corrections are made is inserted to the right of the date of publication or below the date of the new edition, if any. The Admiralty have abandoned this practice since 1972, but it may still be found on some charts that have not been re-issued as a new edition.

Small corrections. At the bottom left hand corner of the chart is the inscription 'Small corrections - '. These are made from information in the Admiralty Notices to Mariners published weekly, monthly, quarterly and annually. The small corrections are entered by hand and the year and number of the small correction is entered on the chart itself in chronological order.

Temporary and Preliminary notices. When charts are received from the Admiralty Chart Depots they are not corrected for any temporary or preliminary notices. This should be done in pencil and the date and number entered chronologically with the small corrections together with (T) or (P) to indicate the type of notice.

COLOURS USED ON CHARTS

All lights, radio beacons and on later charts the tidal stream letters are given a magenta overprint to render them conspicuous.

On the more modern chart areas of sea below certain depths is given a light blue wash or a blue wash line after the appropriate fathom contour. It serves as a warning of shallow water and is used in particular on larger scale charts.

In some positions lights exhibiting coloured sectors are shown. The figure illustrates one such light and the reader is reminded that the arrowed arcs should never be mistaken for the range of visibility of the light.

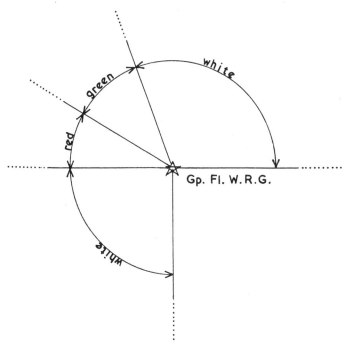

Gp. Fl. W.R.G.

The light shown above shows white from 000° to 090° and from 160° to 270°. The sector from 090° to 120° is red and the sector from 120° to 160° is green. Note that the bearings are always given from seaward and are 'true'.

To distinguish a well surveyed chart the survey should be reasonably modern, the soundings should be close together and regular, depth contour lines should be shown, there should be plenty of detail and the coast line should be complete, a dotted coastline indicates lack of information. It must be remembered that the scale of the chart will govern the number of soundings that can be given.

CHART PUBLISHERS

The most important chart publishers are the hydrographic departments of the major maritime nations. In the UK the Hydrographic Department of the Ministry of Defence, publish the Admiralty Charts which give a detailed, comprehensive coverage of UK and most foreign waters. These excellent charts are designed primarily to be used by large ships and therefore may not always fit the needs of the yachtsman. Consequently, charts of the more popular cruising areas are also published by private chart publishers, such as Stanford Maritime and Imray, Laurie, Norie & Wilson. Such charts are designed specifically for yachtsmen and incorporate much additional inshore information while employing the same cartographic conventions as the Admiralty.

As a rule, it is generally considered wise to use the charts which each maritime nation publishes for its own waters.

METRICATION

Since 1968, the Hydrographic Department has introduced a programme of metrication for its charts. Thus, charts which previously gave depths of water in fathoms and feet and heights above sea level in feet now use metres. This programme is nearing completion in UK waters but there are still areas which are only covered by fathoms charts. Metric charts are greatly improved in appearance and clarity and employ new symbols. It is important that the navigator should be familiar with both of these types of charts.

ABBREVIATIONS

The abbreviations used on charts vary from those contained in the Standard List published by the International Hydrographic Organisation to those in specific use by the Hydrographic Office of the issuing country. In the UK, the symbols and abbreviations used on the Admiralty Charts and detailed on Chart 5011, are closely followed by the private chart publishers. In the U.S.A. and Canada, Chart No. 1 gives similar information.

HINTS ON THE USE OF CHARTS

1. Always use the largest scale chart available because:-
   a. any errors will be reduced to a minimum.
   b. the effect of any distortion will be a minimum.
   c. more detail will be shown.
   d. the plate from which it is printed is corrected before the plates of small scale charts.
2. When transferring a position from one chart to another always use a bearing and distance from a point common to both charts and then check by latitude and longitude.

3. Establish the position of the ship as soon as possible after transferring from another chart.
4. Use the compass rose nearest to the ship's position for courses and bearings as there will be less effect from distortion.
5. Always note the change of variation in the vicinity of the ship's position.
6. Always check and re-check all courses.
7. Make certain that you are using the correct units for interpretation of soundings.
8. Never have more than one chart in use on the chart table to avoid the error of using the wrong latitude scale.
9. When measuring distance, use approximately the same amount on either side of the mean latitude of the track being measured.
10. Use a soft pencil, B or 2B, and a soft eraser as this will preserve the surface of the chart longer.
11. Any times or information which may be written on the chart should be placed astern of the ship's position.
12. Always keep all charts properly corrected from 'Notices to Mariners' and any radio warnings that are received.
13. Charts are an important part of any ship's navigational equipment and should be kept clean and dry, and treated with the utmost respect.

NAUTICAL PUBLICATIONS

CHART CATALOGUE

These catalogues are normally published annually by the various hydrographic authorities and private chart publishers and list the charts and publications which are of use to the navigator.

SAILING DIRECTIONS

Admiralty Sailing Directions cover the world in some 75 volumes. The main contents are:
a. a caution to consult the latest supplement, where these are issued
b. the latest Notices to Mariners incorporated in the book
c. a section dealing with local and national government regulations that affect the mariner
d. information concerning the area covered by the book and the appropriate charts for that area
e. the remainder of the book deals comprehensively with descriptions of the coast lines, harbours, dangers, navigational aids, port facilities, communications, availability of fuel and stores etc.

Pilot Books for popular cruising areas are published by several private publishers. These books contain similar information to that described above, but concentrate principally on providing detailed pilotage information supplemented by large-scale charts and photographs. For example: the Cruising Association Handbook, Scottish West Coast Pilot, The South Coast Harbours, Frisian Pilot, etc.

NAUTICAL ALMANACS

Published annually, these compendiums of nautical information contain high water tables, and information on numerous subjects such as radio aids, radio communication, weather forecasting, safety at sea etc. For example: Reed's Nautical Almanac, Macmillan and Silk Cut Nautical Almanac.

ADMIRALTY LIST OF LIGHTS

Published in 13 volumes covering the world, these give full details of all navigational lights, with a brief description of the structure and fog signal (if any). Volume A covers the British Isles and the North Coast of France.

ADMIRALTY LIST OF RADIO SIGNALS

This is published annually in 6 volumes of which Volume 2 on radio direction finding is most likely to be required by yachtsmen. The *List of Radio Signals for Small Craft* (NP 280) combines selected information from the 6 volumes described above and covers the area from the Kiel Canal to Bordeaux, including the British Isles.

TIDE TABLES

The Admiralty publish 3 volumes covering the world. These give predictions for the year at a number of Standard Ports with additional information to enable predictions to be made at ports classified as Secondary.

Selected tide tables are published in many other publications (see Nautical Almanacs above).

TIDAL STREAM ATLASES

The Admiralty publish 11 of these to cover the Home Waters. These give at a glance, the hourly tidal stream pattern for a specific area. *Stanfords Tidal Atlases* cover the English Channel in 3 volumes. They present hourly tidal stream information supported by a simple and quick method of working out hourly tidal heights.

CORRECTION OF CHARTS

Various publications are made available on a regular basis to keep the mariner informed of the latest changes in navigational aids, dangers to navigation etc.

Notices to Mariners published by many countries, usually on a weekly basis; they contain changes in aids to navigation (lights, buoys, construction work), dangers to navigation (rocks, shoals, banks and sand bars), corrections to radio aids, route information and all such information as affects the yachtsman's charts and other publications, such as List of Lights, List of Radio Signals etc. In the UK, these are published by the Admiralty and are available free on request from Chart Agents.

Small Craft Edition of Notices to Mariners (NP 246) is published quarterly and contains only those Notices which are considered to be of interest to yachtsmen sailing in the area from the Kiel Canal to Bordeaux and including the British Isles.

Correction lists for privately published charts are available on request from the publishers concerned.

On receipt of the appropriate Notice, all charts and publications must be corrected. If the Notice is of a permanent nature, it should be made on the chart in waterproof violet ink in a neat and legible manner. The correction should be made in such a manner so as not to obscure other information. Records should be kept of all Notices received and the action taken, including radio warnings. It is only by diligent application to the task that the yachtsman can insure the accuracy and reliability of his charts.

3
PLOTTING, DEAD RECKONING AND POSITION

THE DIAGRAM illustrates the method of plotting a position that is described by latitude and longitude. The edge of the parallel ruler is placed along a parallel of latitude and then transferred until the edge passes through the required latitude indicated either on the left or right sides of the chart.

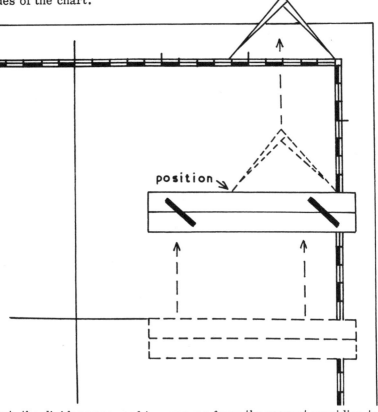

Next, the dividers are used to measure from the nearest meridian to the required longitude at the top or bottom of the chart. This measurement is laid off from the same meridian along the latitude indicated by the edge of the parallel ruler. If it is more convenient the longitude can be indicated by the ruler and the latitude measured by the dividers. A third alternative is to mark the latitude and longitude in pencil using only the parallel rules.

To measure the latitude and longitude of a position on the chart it is often more convenient to use the dividers only as shown in the following figure.

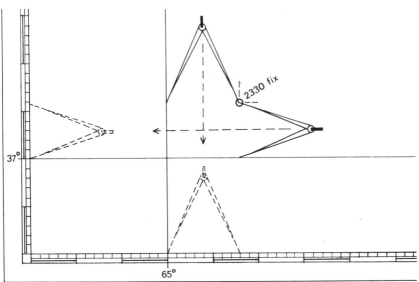

In this method one point of the dividers is placed on the position and the other is adjusted so as to describe an arc that is tangential to the nearest parallel (for latitude) or meridian (for longitude). Without changing the spread of the dividers they are transferred to the appropriate edge of the chart to obtain the latitude or longitude. The objective of describing an arc is to ensure that the perpendicular distance is measured from position to parallel or meridian.

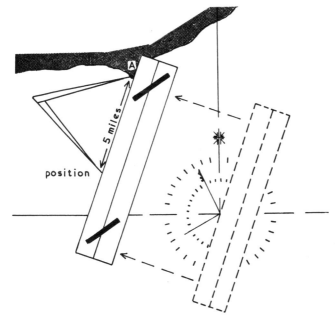

The diagram above shows the method of plotting a position that is described by a bearing and distance from some point. In the example the vessel is bearing 200° distant 5 miles from the lighthouse A. The parallel rules are placed across the nearest compass rose so that one edge cuts the 200° and 020° markings. The ruler is moved until one edge passes through the position of the light. The distance of 5 miles is laid off with the dividers in the direction indicated from the lighthouse, i.e. 200°.

To define a position in terms of bearing and distance the reverse procedure is adopted. The parallel rules are placed so that one edge cuts the light and the position in question and then transferred to the nearest compass rose and the bearing read. Care must be taken to ensure that the correct bearing is read, i.e. from the light, not to the light. The distance is then measured with the dividers.

MEASUREMENT OF DISTANCE

Because of the gradual expansion of the latitude scale northwards in the northern hemisphere (and vice versa in the southern hemisphere) in the Mercator projection, the physical length of a minute of latitude (the nautical mile) will change from the lower part of the chart to the upper. This is very evident of a scale of 1/200,000 and smaller. Distance on the chart must always be measured on the latitude scale abreast of the position as shown in the following diagram.

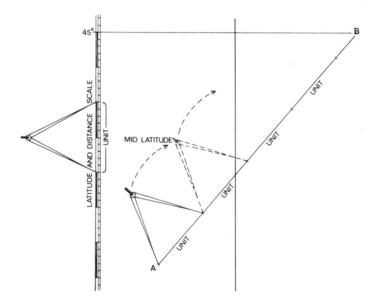

Where the distance to be measured is greater than the normal spread of the dividers, such as with a course line extending over the major part of the chart, a convenient unit (say 10 miles) is selected at the mid-latitude between the two points and the distance then stepped off along the course line. Since this is unlikely to be an exact division of the total distance the residual amount is set on the dividers and measured on the latitude scale.

The preceding remarks apply to all charts on the Mercator projection.

Occasionally, navigators may find themselves using charts on the Polyconic projection and a slightly different technique must be used. This is because the parallels are not straight lines and the meridians angle in toward the pole.

The following diagram illustrates plotting a position on such a chart. The longitude is plotted by placing a straight edge through the appropriate sub-divisions for the longitude required and all or part of the line AA is drawn on the chart. The latitude is set on the dividers and plotted as shown.

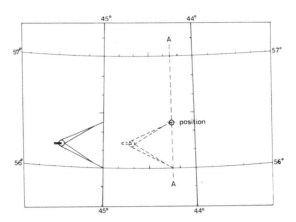

Courses and bearings must be measured at the _nearest_ compass rose to the position of the ship.

POSITION LINES

It is necessary for the navigator to determine whether the vessel is maintaining the required track or course line and he does this by observing visual land marks, utilising radio aids or by observation of celestial bodies. The result of a single observation is known as a position line which may be defined as any line, drawn on the chart, either curved or straight, on which the ship's position is known to lie.

Dead Reckoning (DR)
This term is derived from 'deduced' or 'ded. reckoning' which was the process of deducing or computing the ship's position trigonometrically from a known point of departure. Modern charts permit the solution by graphical methods and the term, in its present form has continued in use. Definitions in dead reckoning vary with text book and with country and have not been standardised. Confusion in terminology can be avoided by remembering that 'course' is direction with reference to the water and that 'track' is direction with reference to the earth.

The following terms and abbreviations are used throughout this book:

Heading (Hdg)   — the horizontal direction in which a ship is heading at any instant.

Course (C)   — a rhumb line direction and horizontal direction of travel through still water, expressed in angular measure using the 3 figure notation. Course may be designated true, magnetic, compass or gyro depending on the reference direction.

Course line	— the graphic representation of the ship's course used in the construction of a DR plot.
Track (Tr)	— the rhumb line or lines describing the path of a vessel over the ground. This is often referred to as the 'course made good' (CMG).
Intended track (ITr)	— the anticipated path of the vessel over the ground after considering the estimated effects of wind and current.
Speed (S)	— the rate of movement through the water, expressed in knots. It may be indicated by means of a log or may be calculated from the engine revolutions.
Speed made good (SMG)	— the ship's actual speed over the ground along the track.
Speed of advance (SOA)	— the average speed to maintain in order to arrive at a point at a certain time.
DR position	— the ship's position as determined from a vector or series of vectors using *only the true course and the speed through the water.*
Estimated position (EP)	— the best estimate of the ship's position after consideration is made of the effects of wind, current, etc. In effect it is the DR position modified by the best information available.
Estimated time of arrival (ETA)	— the best estimate of the arrival time at any specific point.
DR plot	— it is the graphical representation on the chart of the true course or courses and indicated speeds from a known position. It may represent courses and speeds to be used or that have previously been used. It must be correctly labelled with courses, speeds and times indicating various DR positions.

Labelling on the chart

Methods of labelling courses, speeds and positions on the chart vary from text to text: the essential point is that the labelling must be clearly understood by everybody participating in the navigation of the ship.

The following system, based on the Admiralty method, has been used throughout this book.

SYMBOL	SIGNIFICANCE
	Dead reckoning position with time
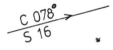	Estimated position with time
	Fix and method
C 078° / S 16	Course line and speed in knots
ITr 125° / SOA 12.5	Intended track and speed of advance (knots)
	Single position line (LOP) with time

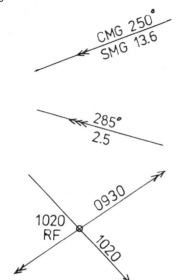

Course and speed made good

Set (direction) and rate of current
or tidal stream

Position line from earlier reckoning,
transferred to form running fix
with later position line

PLOTTING A COURSE

The course from one place to another on the chart is found by laying one edge of the parallel rules so that it passes through the two places and then transferring the parallel rule to the nearest compass rose to obtain the true course. The reciprocal reading should also be noted so that any distortion can be detected. Remember that if the inner rose is used the resultant course will be the magnetic course subject to the correction of the variation for the current year.

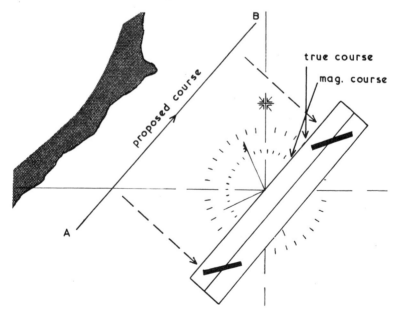

The diagram above shows the use of the parallel ruler in determining the course between A and B on the chart using the compass rose. This method is preferable to using the meridian which does not permit the detection of distortion. The lower diagram shows the procedure if the meridian is used. In this case the south index (or 90° index if the course is required in points) is aligned with the meridian and the course or bearing is read on the opposite graduated edge.

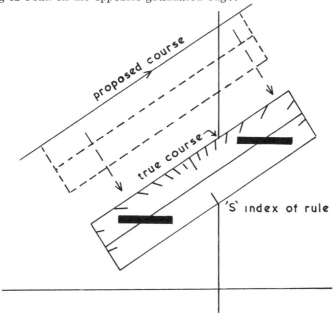

The following are the principal rules that should be observed in chartwork:

- immediately after drawing any line or plotting any point on the chart, label it
- the label for a point should make an angle away from the line
- the label indicating direction along a course line should lie above and along the line
- speed, where indicated, should lie along the course line and immediately below the direction label
- never obscure information of navigational importance when labelling
- always print all labels neatly and clearly
- always maintain a DR plot. The means of fixing the ship's position may not always be available due to weather or equipment failure, etc. If conditions were ideal, i.e. no wind or current effects, the steering was perfect and no other factors affected the ship's progress through the water, the DR position would be accurate. Since these conditions rarely exist, the DR indicates an approximation of the position and in the absence of other information must be used to determine when to alter course, predict the times of sighting navigational aids and identifying landmarks.

The frequency of plotting DR positions will depend on the prevailing circumstances and the scale of the chart in use. It may vary from hourly on coastal charts to 12 hour intervals on small scale ocean charts. A DR position should be plotted for each course change.

32

WIND

The effect of the wind on a vessel's movement through the water is two-fold. Firstly it will cause an increase or decrease of the speed through the water depending whether the wind is abaft or forward of the beam, respectively. The resultant velocity through the water will be recorded by the log but if the vessel's speed is calculated from engine revolutions due allowance must be made for the effect of the wind. Secondly the wind produces a sailing effect from the vessel's superstructure. In general the vessel will be moved bodily to leeward, the amount will vary with trim and the general design of the upperworks. The angle between the ship's fore and aft line and the direction made good is termed the 'leeway'. It is assessed by visually estimating the angle between the fore and aft line and the wake - not a reliable method.

The diagram shows the effect of the wind on the vessel's track. Note that the ship's head indicates the direction steered but that her progress is in the direction made good.

Where it is required to make good a particular course the leeway must be applied into the wind. Normally leeway is not plotted on the chart, only the resultant path, known as the leeway track.

Worked Example

Find the course made good (leeway track) from the following information: compass course 228°, variation 10° W., wind SE causing an estimated leeway of 7°. Use the deviation card in Chapter 1.

Deviation for 228° C.

220° C.	dev.	11° E
230° C.	dev.	$8\frac{1}{2}°$ E
10°		$2\frac{1}{2}°$

required dev. $= 11° - (\frac{5}{2} \times \frac{8}{10})$

$= 9°$ E

compass course	228°
deviation	9° E
magnetic course	237°
variation	10° W
true course	227°
leeway	7°
leeway track	234°

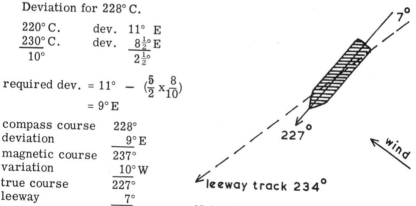

Note: the direction of the wind is the direction from which it is blowing.

Worked Example
Find the compass course to steer to make good a true course of 335°
given that a westerly wind is causing 6° leeway. Variation 9°W. Deviation table from Chapter 1.

Deviation for 338° M

leeway track	335°
leeway	6°
true course	329°
variation	9°W
magnetic course	338°
deviation	14°W
compass course	352°

350° C.	dev.	15°W	335° M
360° C.	dev.	10°W	350° M
		5°	15°

required dev. $= 15° - (\frac{5}{15} \times \frac{3}{1})$

$= 14°W$

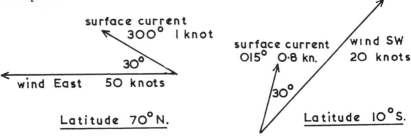

leeway track 335°

329°

6°

wind

THE EFFECT OF WIND IN PRODUCING CURRENT

A further effect of the wind on a vessel's track is to produce a surface
current that is unrelated to the existing tidal stream or current. The
full strength of the current is apparent after the wind has blown steadily
for at least 24 hours. Its rate is about 2% of the wind speed in high
latitudes and about 4% in low latitudes. The direction of this surface
current, in the northern hemisphere, is some 30° to the right of the
direction in which the wind is blowing and to the left in the southern
hemisphere.

surface current
300° 1 knot

30°

wind East   50 knots

Latitude 70°N.

surface current
015° 0·8 kn.

wind SW
20 knots

30°

Latitude 10°S.

It must be borne in mind that these figures apply to open deep waters
and the effect of the wind in producing surface currents can be considerably reduced by shallow water and the effect of the adjacent coastline.

CURRENTS

Currents are permanent or seasonal horizontal movements of the surface of the oceans. The information concerning their direction and strength is given on charts, in Sailing Directions and in various current atlases. The net result is a uniform movement of the water in a given direction that transports a vessel bodily without affecting the ship's head.

TIDAL STREAMS

These are horizontal movements of the water that result from the tide raising forces and must not be confused with ocean currents although their immediate effect is the same. Tidal streams are of two main classes, rectilinear and rotatory. The former has only two directions normally called ebb and flood, the latter continually changes direction through $360°$ in a complete cycle. Information concerning tidal streams is given on Admiralty charts, Sailing Directions and in special tidal stream atlases that cover various parts of the world.

SET. This is the direction that a given current or tidal stream is moving, e.g. a current that is setting 265° will cause a vessel to be carried in the direction 265°.

RATE. This is the velocity of the current or tidal stream and is always expressed in knots.

DRIFT. This is the distance that a given current or tidal stream will move in a given interval of time.

A vessel that experiences a current setting 150°, rate 3 knots, will be set 150° and she will drift 3 miles in one hour.

When a vessel is affected by a current or tidal stream, its movement over the bottom will be in the resultant of two vectors:

— the course and speed through the water of the vessel
— the direction and rate of the current.

The following diagram illustrates the current triangle. The terminology for the parts of the triangle are dependent on whether the current is estimated or true.

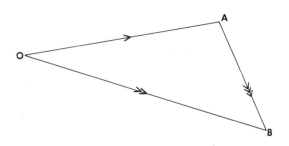

THE TIDAL STREAM OR CURRENT TRIANGLE

PART OF TRIANGLE	USING AN ESTIMATED CURRENT	USING ACTUAL CURRENT
Point 0 Point A Point B	Present position (fix) of ship DR position at future time Estimated position at future time	Previous position (fix) of ship DR position at present time Present position (fix) of ship
Side 0A Side 0B Side AB	Course and speed vector Intended track and SOA Estimated current	Course and speed vector CMG and SMG vector Actual current experienced

ALLOWING FOR A CURRENT

Worked Example

At noon, a ship is fixed at position A (see diagram below) and is steering a course of 105°T. and the log speed is 10 knots. The current is known to set 049°T. at 2 knots. Plot the vessel's estimated position at 1400.

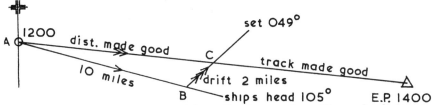

The true course steered is laid from the observed position and a distance equal to one hour's speed is measured along this line AB. The current is laid off from B in the direction given and a distance equal to one hour's rate is measured from B - BC. The line AC represents the course and distance made good by the ship in one hour i.e. it is the track. To find the E.P. at 1400, AC is extended the same amount and in the same direction.

ALLOWING FOR A CURRENT AND LEEWAY

Worked Example

At 1600, the observed position was at A. True course 036°. Tidal stream 142°T. rate 3 knots. Wind NW causing an estimated 8° leeway. If the log was 100 at 1600 and 125 at 1800 plot the E.P.

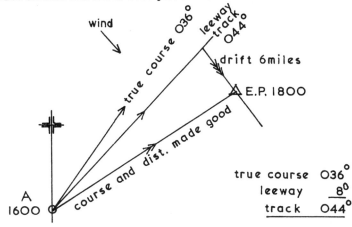

true course	036°
leeway	8°
track	044°

The procedure is the same as for the previous example except that the log distance must be measured along the leeway track. The total distance was laid along the leeway track but one hour's distance could have been measured ($12\frac{1}{2}$ miles) and the resultant track extended by the same amount to obtain the E.P. at 1600.

Note: the true course has been shown on the diagram but in practice this is omitted and the leeway course laid direct.

TO COUNTERACT A GIVEN CURRENT

Worked Example

A vessel wishes to make good a course of 255°T. If the tidal stream is setting 300°T. at 3 knots find the true course to steer if the speed of the ship is 12 knots.

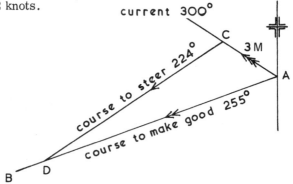

The first step is to lay off the course to be made good AB. From A lay off the direction of the tidal stream. AC is the distance that the tidal stream sets in any convenient interval, say 1 hour (AC = 3 miles). With centre C and radius equal to the distance run by the ship in the same period of time (12 miles) intersect AB at D. CD is the required course to steer and the distance along AB in one hour would be AD.

The method outlined above is based on the parallelogram of velocities which states:

If a moving body possesses two simultaneous velocities represented in magnitude and direction by the lines OA and OB, (see diagram below) they are equivalent to a velocity represented by the diagonal OC of the parallelogram OACB.

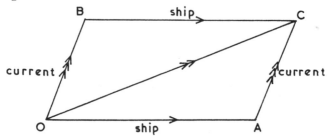

In the parallelogram OA represents the direction and speed of the ship while OB represents the direction and speed of the current, hence the resultant direction and speed OC is the course and speed made good. From a practical point of view, it is only necessary to draw the triangle OBC.

Note: triangle OAC gives the solution of allowing for a given current.

COUNTERACTING BOTH CURRENT AND LEEWAY
Worked Example
Find the course to steer (true) to make good 100° T. Current setting 175°
at 2 knots. Wind NE causing an estimated leeway of 6°. Log speed 13
knots.

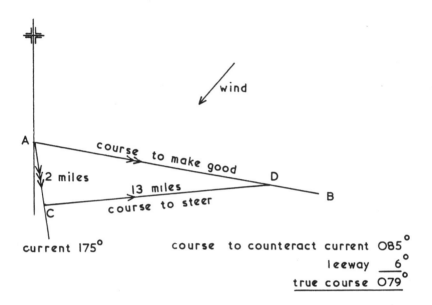

Note: the course to steer is plotted on the chart as for normal counter-
action of current and the leeway is applied afterwards into the wind.

TO REACH A POSITION AT A DEFINITE TIME

Worked Example
A vessel obtains a fix at A and requires to reach B four hours later.
The tidal stream is setting 047° T. at 2 knots. Maximum speed of vessel
11 knots.

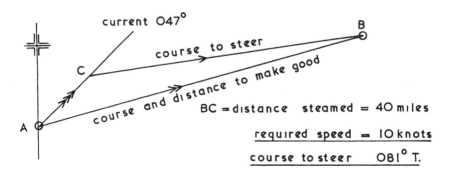

Join AB, this gives the course and distance to be made good in 4 hours. From A lay off the direction of the current (047° T.) and the drift for 4 hours (8 miles) AC. Join BC. This is the course to steer to make B and the distance BC divided by 4 gives the speed necessary to reach B at the required time.

This problem may arise in practice where it is necessary to make a port in daylight, or where a pilot will be waiting for the ship at a certain time.

TO FIND THE TIME TO REACH A GIVEN POINT

Worked Example

A vessel in position A wishes to pass 3 miles off the lightship B, the current is setting 312° T. at 3 knots. Speed of vessel 12 knots. Find the course to steer and the time the lightship will be abeam.

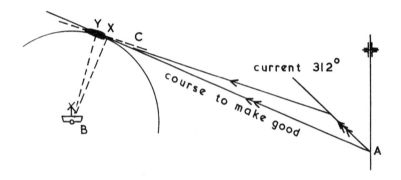

An arc of radius 3 miles is drawn on the side of the lightship it is wished to pass. A tangent from A to this arc gives the course to make good. The current is counteracted as previously explained - in this case both ship and current distances are for one hour - AC is the distance made good in one hour and this must be divided into the total distance to find the time that will elapse.

Note: since the term 'abeam' is relative to ship's head, the point when the lightship is abeam is at Y not at X.

TO FIND THE TRUE SET AND DRIFT

As so often happens, information regarding an existing set may be scanty and although a particular current may be allowed for, subsequent obser-vations may show that the ship has been displaced from the intended track. The problem is to find the set and drift actually experienced.

Worked Example

A vessel in position A wishes to make good a course to reach B, the current is estimated to set 136° T. at 2 knots. Speed of vessel through the water is 10 knots. After running for 3 hours a fix was obtained at C. Find the true set and drift.

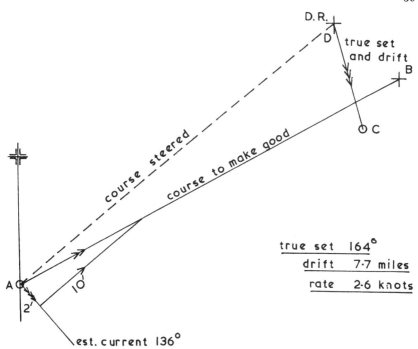

true set 164°

drift 7·7 miles

rate 2·6 knots

In this type of problem the current is counteracted as before; however, when the second fix shows that the allowance is erroneous it becomes necessary to ascertain the D.R. at the time of the second observation in order to determine the actual set and drift.

The course steered to counteract the estimated current is laid off from the starting position A and the distance run by the vessel through the water is measured along this line. This gives the D.R. position D as though there was no current. Since the observed position is at C then DC must be the actual set and drift experienced.

TO FIND THE TRUE SET AND DRIFT WITH LEEWAY
Worked Example

A vessel in position A wishes to pass 5 miles off point P. The current is assumed to set 248° T at 3 knots and a NW wind is causing an estimated 7° leeway. Speed of vessel 11 knots. After running for two hours a fix gave the position of the ship at B. Find the actual set and drift.

The addition of leeway does not complicate the issue, it is still necessary to find the E.P. allowing for leeway but no current at the time of the fix. The allowance for leeway, in the absence of any further information, must be assumed to be correct.

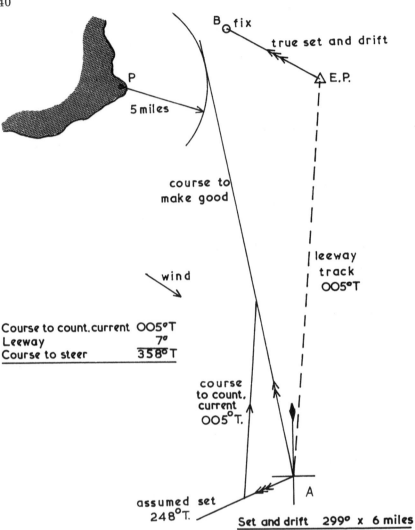

Course to count.current OO5°T
Leeway   7°
Course to steer   358°T

TO ARRIVE AT A POSITION WITH A GIVEN POINT x° ON THE BOW
   AT A GIVEN DISTANCE
Worked Example
It is required to reach a position from A such that point P will be 20° on
the starboard bow at a distance of 15 miles.

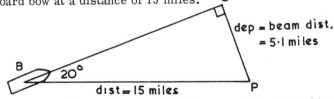

In the diagram above it can be seen that if the vessel is at B and heading in the direction BC, then point P will be 20° on the starboard bow at a distance equal to PB. Triangle PBC is right angled at C and the distance PC can be found from the Traverse Table.

Entering Traverse Table with angle on bow as 'course' and required distance the 'departure' = PC = 5.1 miles.

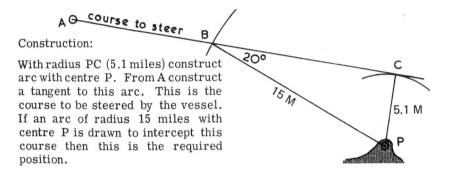

Construction:

With radius PC (5.1 miles) construct arc with centre P. From A construct a tangent to this arc. This is the course to be steered by the vessel. If an arc of radius 15 miles with centre P is drawn to intercept this course then this is the required position.

TO ARRIVE WITH A GIVEN POINT RIGHT AHEAD AT EXTREME RANGE
Worked Example

An observer on board ship at A wishes to arrive off the light P at its extreme range and with the light right ahead. Current setting 164° at 3 knots. Speed of vessel 12 knots. Observer's height of eye 40'. What is the true course to steer?

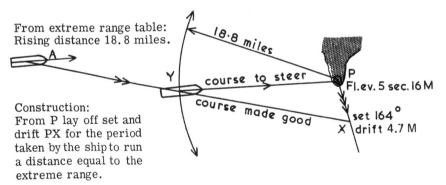

From extreme range table:
Rising distance 18.8 miles.

Construction:
From P lay off set and drift PX for the period taken by the ship to run a distance equal to the extreme range.

$$\frac{18.8}{12} \times 3 = 4.7 \quad \text{i.e. set and drift} = 164° \times 4.7 \text{ miles.}$$

Join AX, this is the track made good by the vessel which intersects the extreme range arc at Y.

Join YP, this is the course to be steered by the vessel in order to arrive on the extreme range arc with P right ahead.

4
OBTAINING A POSITION LINE

A POSITION LINE has already been defined as a straight or curved line on the chart on which the ship's position is known to lie. The following are the methods of obtaining a position line from terrestrial objects only.

A VISUAL COMPASS BEARING

All standard compasses on merchant ships are fitted with a device to assist in the taking of visual bearings known as an azimuth circle. The resultant position line is known as a line of bearing. If the magnetic compass is used the bearing must be corrected for the error of the ship's head.

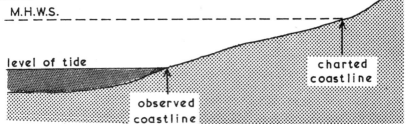

When taking a bearing of the edge of land it must be remembered that the charted coastline refers to Mean High Water Springs and if the land is not vertical the position line will be in error.

A RELATIVE BEARING

The line of bearing is obtained in this method by simply noting the direction of the object relative to the ship's head. In order to plot the line of bearing on the chart the relative bearing must be applied to the true heading.

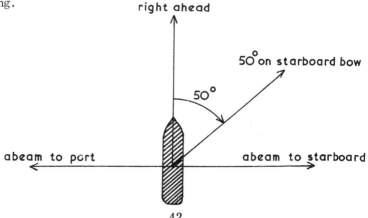

Worked Example

The navigator on a yacht observes the light A to be bearing 50° on the starboard
bow. If the compass course is 326° and the total error of the compass is 25°E.
determine the true bearing to be plotted on the chart.

Course	326°C.
Error	25°E.
Course	351°T.
Relative bearing	50°
Bearing	041°T.

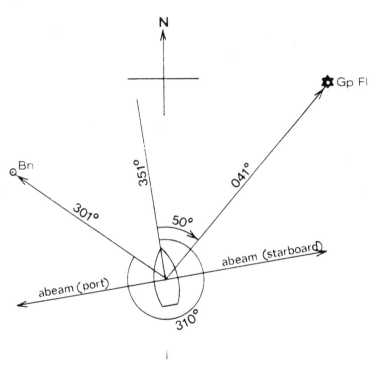

Note
Relative bearings may be given in three figure notation measured clockwise from
the ship's head. In this case they will always be added to the true course to
obtain the true bearing, i.e. the beacon shown in the diagram above has a relative
bearing of 310° (or 50° on port bow). Therefore the true bearing is 351° (true
course) + 310° = 661° or 301°T.

A TRANSIT

When two objects are observed in line, they are said to be in transit and
the observer must be situated on the extension of the line joining them.
Provided the distance of the observer from the nearer object is not more
than about three times the distance separating the objects the results are
usually good.

A transit affords an excellent method of checking the error of the

44

compass by comparing the compass bearing of the transit and the true bearing as indicated by the chart.

Diagram illustrating a transit

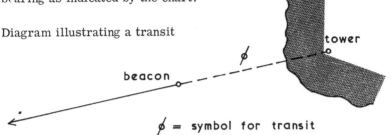

ϕ = symbol for transit

A transit affords an excellent method of checking the error of the compass for the ship's head at the time of observation. The error is obtained by comparison of the observed bearing of the transit with the true bearing indicated on the chart. The competent navigator must be able to detect from the chart objects that will make good transits, particularly when manoeuvered in restricted waters.

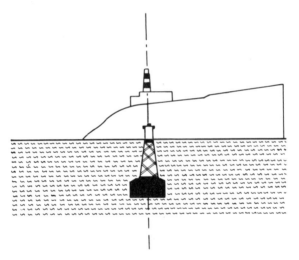

lighthouse and buoy in transit

HORIZON RANGES

The more common name for this method of obtaining a position line is 'dipping distance'. The method is used at night for finding the distance off a light as it rises above, or dips below the horizon. The observer must know the physical height of the light and his own eye above sea level. The distance of the horizon for various heights can be found from Navigation Tables (Norie's, Burton's), the List of Lights or from Lecky's Tables.

Most tables utilise the Admiralty formula:

Distance of sea horizon (miles) = $1.15\sqrt{\text{height in feet}}$
or $2.08\sqrt{\text{height in metres}}$

this formula applies under normal conditions of refraction, if abnormal conditions are suspected this method should be avoided.

The tables also include Extreme Range Tables which combine the above formula so that the navigator enters the table with his own height of eye and the height of the light to obtain the extreme range that the light may be seen.

However, these tables and formulae depend on the light being powerful enough to be seen through the conditions of visibility that prevail at the time.

When conditions of visibility are suspect, the range of a light may be determined from a nominal range diagram found in the Light Lists.

Geographic Range — This is determined as explained previously and is the visible range of an object by virtue of its physical height only.

Computed Range — Synonomous for Geographic Range.

Luminous Range — The theoretical distance that a light may be seen due to its power under conditions of perfect visibility.

Nominal Range — The visible range of a light under conditions of visibility of 10 miles and is in fact, a particular case of Luminous Range.

Visible Range — The actual range of the light due to prevailing conditions of visibility in the area between the observer and the light.

Note: Earlier charts indicated the visibility of a light as that for an observer with a height of 15 feet. Modern charts indicate the *nominal* range of a light.

The following diagram illustrates the various ranges for an observer with a height of eye of 20m and a light with a height of 60m and a luminous range of 30 miles.

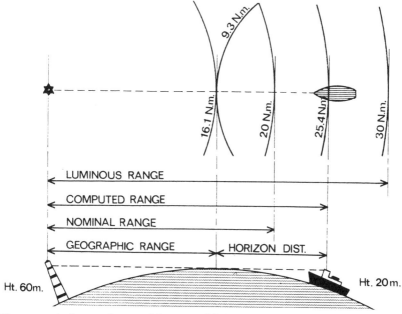

The computed range (geographic range of light plus horizon distance of observer) is 25.4 miles.

If the visibility is 10 miles then the nominal range will be 20 miles and the observer will not see the light until he is 20 miles from it.

If the visibility is 5 miles (refer to Nominal Range Diagram) then the observer will not see the light until he is just under 12 miles from it.

If the computed range exceeds the luminous range of a light it will not be seen until the observer reaches the luminous range.

Worked Example

An observer, height of eye 36 feet, observes a light dip below the horizon, Height of light 169 feet. Find the distance off.

From Burton's Tables: From the formula:

height 169 feet - distance 14.95 miles $1.15\sqrt{169}$........ = 14.95 miles
height 36 feet - distance 6.9 miles $1.15\sqrt{36}$ .... = 6.9 miles
distance from light $\overline{21.85}$ miles   distance from light $\overline{21.85}$ miles

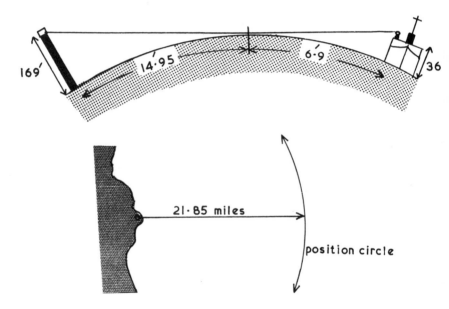

Note: the position of the ship can be fixed if a bearing of the light is taken at the time of rising or dipping. The observer should remember that the charted heights of lights are above M.H.W.S. and if extreme accuracy is required due allowance must be made for the height of the tide.

Worked Example

The light shown in the diagram was observed to rise bearing 240° C. Vessel steering 170° C. Error 12° W. Plot the vessel's position if the height of the observer's eye is 40'.

Note: In this example it is necessary to use the charted range of the light which is given for a height of eye of 15'. As the observer has a greater height of eye the position will be further from the light and the correct distance must be found. The power of the light is taken into account when giving the range and consequently the charted range may differ from that found by using the charted height of a light.

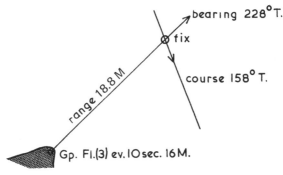

bearing 228°T.

fix

course 158°T.

range 18.8 M

Gp. Fl.(3) ev. 10 sec. 16 M.

Using Extreme Range Table:
Entering with height of eye 15' follow the column downwards to a range of 16 miles. Proceed horizontally to find the correct distance off under height of eye 40' i.e. 18.8 miles.

Using Distance to Sea Horizon Tables:

Charted range	16.0 miles
Distance of sea horizon for 15'	4.45 miles
Distance visible at sea level	11.55 miles
Distance of sea horizon for 40'	7.3 miles
Distance light visible from 40'	18.85 miles

VERTICAL SEXTANT ANGLES

If the angle subtended by a vertical object is measured, the solution of a right angled triangle will give the distance from the base of the object. This principle can be extended to terrestrial objects seen at sea, the vertical angle subtended by them at the observer is measured with a sextant.

The resultant triangle can be solved manually or by utilising the vertical sextant tables in most navigation tables.

Worked Example

The vertical sextant angle of a lighthouse, height 240 feet, is observed as 00° 44'.0. Find the distance off.

From Burton's Tables, entered with height 240 feet and angle 00° 44'.0 the resulting distance is given as 3.1 miles. The position line will be the circumference of a circle radius 3.1 miles around the light.

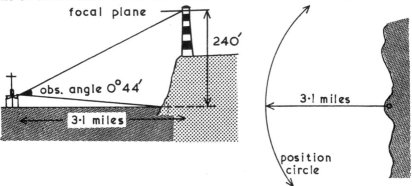

focal plane

240'

obs. angle 0° 44'

3.1 miles

3.1 miles

position circle

The assumptions made are:
1. the observed triangle is right angled,
2. there are no effects from refraction,
3. the surface of the Earth is flat,
4. the height of the observer's eye is nil,
5. the foreshore is vertically below the object.

Note: the charted height is given from the focal plane (centre of lens) to the level of M.H.W.S. so due allowance must be made for the tide.

The manual solution of the above is:

$$\frac{\text{distance off in miles x 6080}}{\text{height of object in feet}} = \text{cotan. observed angle}$$

$$\text{therefore distance off in miles} = \frac{\text{cotan. observed angle x height of object}}{6080}$$

log. cotan 00° 44!0	1.893
log 240	2.380
	4.273
log 6080	3.784
log distance off	0.489

therefore the distance off = 3.08 miles

HORIZONTAL ANGLES

If an observer measures the horizontal angle subtended by two objects that are marked on the chart it is possible for the circle of position to be plotted.

The horizontal angle can be measured with a sextant which gives the greatest accuracy, or by means of the difference between the compass bearings of the objects. This latter method may be used even if the compass error is not known, since it must be the same for both bearings. The horizontal angle could also be determined by noting the relative bearings of the objects, the difference between them being the horizontal angle.

The plotting is based on two geometrical propositions:
1. the angle subtended by a chord at the centre of a circle is twice the angle subtended at the circumference.

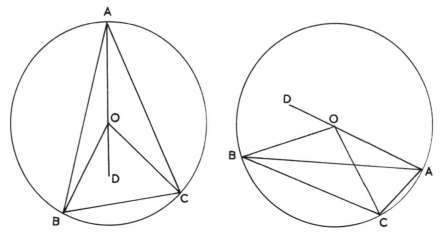

Let ABC be any circle with O as the centre; let BOC be the angle subtended by the chord BC at the centre of the circle, and BAC the angle
subtended by the same chord at the circumference.

Join AO and produce this line to D,

In triangle OAB, since OB = OA	=	radius
then angle OAB	=	angle OBA (isosceles triangle)
therefore angle OAB + angle OBA	=	twice angle OAB,
but the exterior angle BOD	=	angle OAB + angle OBA
therefore the exterior angle BOD	=	twice angle OAB
similarly, angle DOC	=	twice angle OAC

by adding the results in the left hand figure and taking the difference in
the right hand figure it follows in each case that:

<u>the angle BOC = twice the angle BAC</u>

2. the angles in the same segment of a circle are equal.

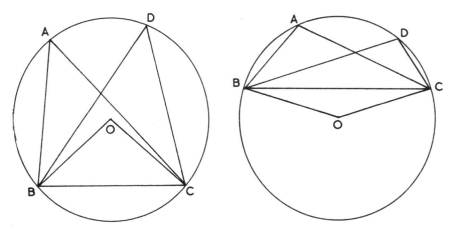

Let BAC, BDC be angles in the same segment BADC of a circle whose
centre is at O.

Join BO and OC
since angle BOC is at the centre and angle BAC is at the circumference on the same arc BC,
therefore the angle BOC = twice the angle BAC
similarly the angle BOC = twice the angle BDC
<u>therefore the angle BAC = the angle BDC</u>

The diagram illustrates the construction of the position circle when the
measured angle is less than 90°.

50

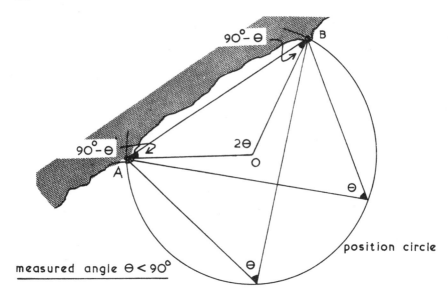

The line joining AB is the chord of the position circle.

The complement of the measured angle is laid off to seaward, i.e. the vessel lies somewhere on the major segment.

With O as centre and OA or OB as radius the circle of position is completed.

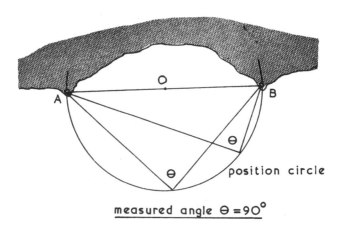

When the measured angle is equal to 90° the chord joining AB is the diameter of the position circle.

O is the mid-point of AB; with centre O and radius OA or OB complete the circle of position.

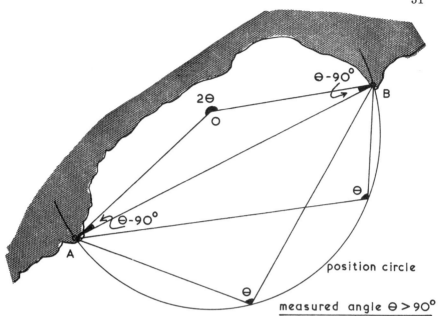

measured angle Θ > 90°

When the measured angle is greater than 90° the observer will lie some-where on the minor segment.

In this case the excess of the measured angle over 90° is laid off on AB away from the observer.

With centre O and radius OA or OB complete the position circle.

USING THE HORIZONTAL ANGLE AS A DANGER ANGLE

This type of danger angle requires two well charted objects identified by the navigator and which subtend a substantial horizontal angle.

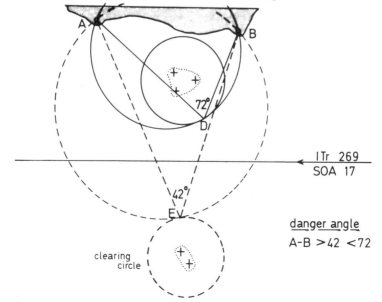

danger angle
A-B >42 <72

The above figure represents a portion of the coastline with two off lying shoals between which the navigator wishes to pass. A and B are two clearly identified objects, both visually and on the chart.

Clearing circles are drawn around the shoals allowing a safety margin for the ship to manoeuvre should an emergency arise. Circles are then drawn tangential to the clearing circles and passing through A and B.

The tangent points (E and D) are then joined to A and B and the angles ADB and AEB are measured.

The navigator should then note on the chart the limiting danger angles.

In this case the horizontal angle subtended by A and B must not be less than $42°$ or greater than $72°$ in order to ensure that the vessel safely clears the two shoals.

A single horizontal danger angle may be used to clear an off lying danger.

USING THE VERTICAL ANGLE AS A DANGER ANGLE

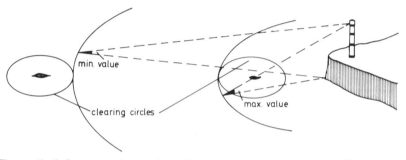

The vertical danger angle involves the same general principles as illustrated in the above figure in which AB represents a vertical object of known height.

The prudent navigator must be aware of the effect of the tidal height at the time of passage and also that small vertical angles are very sensitive, i.e. a significant change in the distance off occurs with only a very small change in the vertical angle.

TO FIND THE MAXIMUM ANGLE SUBTENDED BY TWO POINTS TO A
    GIVEN COURSE LINE.
Worked Example
A vessel is steering along the track (AB in the diagram). It is required to know the maximum angle subtended by points P and Q.

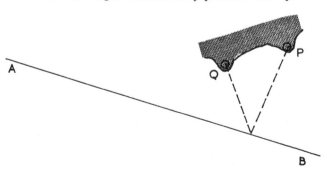

Method 1

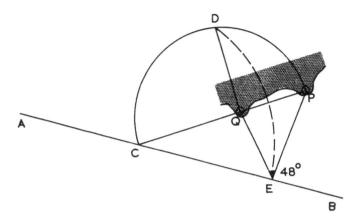

Join PQ and produce this line to meet AB at C.
Find the mid-point of PC and construct semi-circle PDC.
Construct a perpendicular to PC at Q to intersect semi-circle at D.
With centre C and radius CD construct arc DE.
E is the position where points P and Q subtend the maximum horizontal angle to line AB.

Method 2

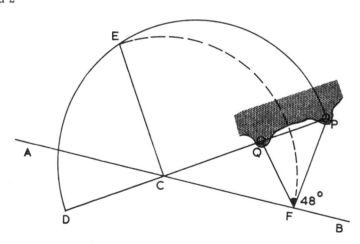

Join PQ and produce this line to intersect AB at C continuing to D such that CD = QC.
On PD construct a semi-circle PED and erect perpendicular CE.
Construct CF equal to CE.
F is the position where points P and Q subtend the maximum horizontal angle to line AB.

54

Method 3 (trial and error)

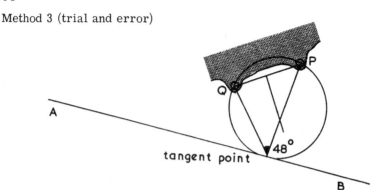

Construct the perpendicular bisector to PQ. This is the locus line of all circles passing through PQ.

The 'trial and error' is necessary to construct a circle that passes through PQ and is also tangential to AB.

Where this circle is tangential to AB is the position where points P and Q subtend the maximum horizontal angle to line AB.

5
FIXING THE POSITION

A FIX, by definition, is the intersection of two or more position lines obtained simultaneously from known positions. If simultaneous observations cannot be made, one or more of the position lines must be transferred in the direction and for the distance travelled by the vessel in the time interval given, to give a running fix.

TRANSFERRING A POSITION LINE

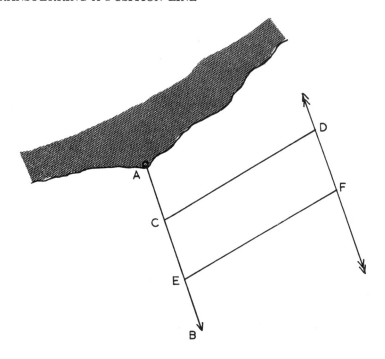

In the diagram AB represents a position line obtained by visual bearing or other means available to the navigator. After obtaining the position line the vessel runs in the direction and for the distance indicated by CD. If the vessel was at C then at the end of the time she would be at D, however, if the vessel was at E then at the end of the interval she would be at F. Clearly a line drawn through DF will be in the same direction as the original position line AB. DF is the position line transferred and should be indicated by double arrowheads as shown.

USE OF A SINGLE POSITION LINE

When the navigator is unable to obtain a fix, a single LOP can be utilised to obtain a most probable position in conjunction with the DR position at the time of the LOP.

The DR position at the time of observation represents the best position in the absence of other information. When plotted, the LOP represents the loci of all possible points the ship could have occupied at the time of the observation. The most probable position (it could be termed EP) of the ship would be that point on the LOP which is closest to the DR position.

Worked Example

A vessel is steering 064°T at a speed of 15 knots. A single observation of light P is obtained at 0340 bearing 294°T. Plot the EP of the vessel.

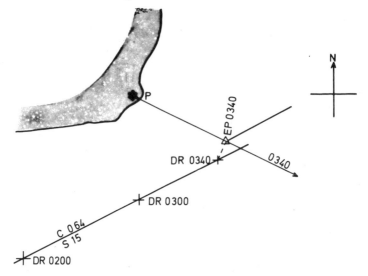

The course is plotted and the DR run up to the time of observation (0340). The LOP is plotted and a perpendicular constructed from the LOP to the DR. The intersection of this perpendicular and the LOP is the EP of the vessel, labelled as shown. The intended track should be plotted from this point.

A second use of the single LOP is to enable the navigator to make a given point, or to clear a danger without other information being immediately available. By transferring the LOP to some point where it may become the intended track the navigator can remove some of the element of doubt that may exist when a fix cannot be obtained.

Worked Example

A vessel is on course 080°T at a speed of 10 knots in foggy weather.

At 2300 a single bearing (345°T) is obtained of the light P. The current is estimated to set 130° at 3 knots.

Course is to be altered when clear of the point in a northerly direction.

Plot the intended track to clear the shoal east of the point.

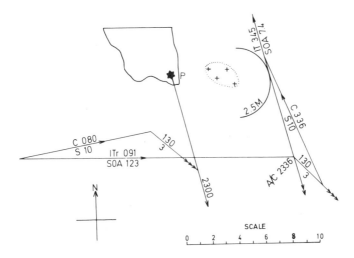

The LOP is plotted from the light and the present intended track laid through the LOP at any point. Using the LOP as the next intended track plot this to ensure safe clearance of the shoal. The speed of advance will determine the time to alter course. The course to steer to make the intended track must consider the effects of the estimated current.

THE RUNNING FIX

This method of fixing the ship's position can be used to advantage when it is impossible to obtain simultaneous position lines.

The two position lines are obtained at different times and the fix is made by transferring the first position line to the time of taking the second position line. The point of intersection is the ship's position at the time of the second observation.

RUNNING FIX WITHOUT CURRENT

Worked Example

At 0900 the lighthouse (A) bore 320°T and at 1000 it bore 015°T. Course 247°T and speed 12 knots.
Plot the fix at 1000.

Any point may be selected on the 1st LOP and the vessel's course and speed between bearings plotted from this point (247° X 12 miles). The first LOP is transferred to this point.

The fix is the intersection of the second LOP and the transferred LOP. This should be labelled as shown and the vessel's intended track plotted from this point. In practice, the point selected on the first LOP would be the intersection of the course line and the LOP.

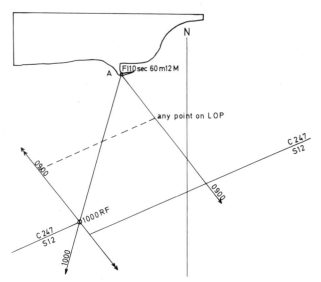

RUNNING FIX WITH ESTIMATED CURRENT

Worked Example

A vessel steering 249° T. at 12 knots observes point P to bear 320° T. and one hour later P bore 021° T. Tidal stream setting 175° T at 3 knots and a NNW wind is causing 5° leeway. Find the ship's position at the time of the second bearing.

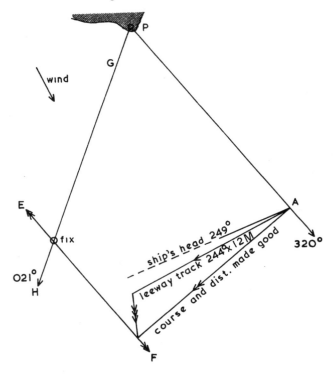

In the diagram the course and distance made good is plotted from A which is any point on the first bearing. The intersection of the transferred position line EF with the second bearing GH is the fix.

Note: the location of the fix is entirely dependent on the accurate knowledge of the course and distance made good by the ship. Should this information be in error then the resultant fix will also be in error.

It is not necessary for the second position line to be obtained from the same object since the change in the bearing may not produce a good angle of cut.

The following diagram illustrates this point. P is the first point used for the initial position line, Q is the point used for the second position line. Note that the second bearing of P would have produced a narrow angle of cut, the nearer this angle is to 90° the better the indication of the position.

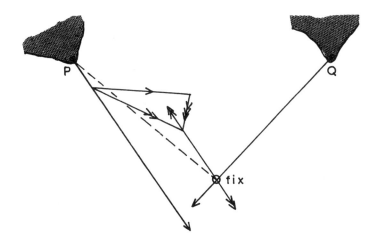

RUNNING FIX WITH UNKNOWN CURRENT

The following example illustrates how the presence of a current may be detected.

Worked Example

While on course 109°T at a speed of 15 knots the following bearings of point P were obtained:

0910	069°T	0920	040°T	0942	318°T

Plot a running fix for all bearings to detect the presence of any current.

The first running fix is plotted from 0910 to 0920 and shows the vessel to the south of the track (2.5 miles run). The second running fix is plotted from 0920 to 0942 and shows the vessel to the north of the track (5.5 miles run). The third running fix is plotted from 0910 to 0942 and shows a conflict with the 0920 to 0942 running fix. (8.0 miles run).

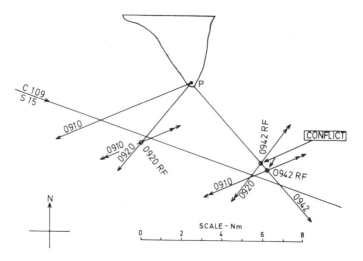

Under these circumstances the approach is to use the last known position of the vessel. However, care must be taken as the running fix still depends on all conditions having remained constant from the time of the last known position. It would be futile to use a fix that had been obtained the day before.

Worked Example

At 1900 the position of the vessel was fixed by celestial observations, A on the diagram. Course 108°T and speed 10 knots. At 2030 the light X bore 050°T and at 2200 the same light bore 000°T. Plot the position at 2200 and show the set and drift experienced since 1900.

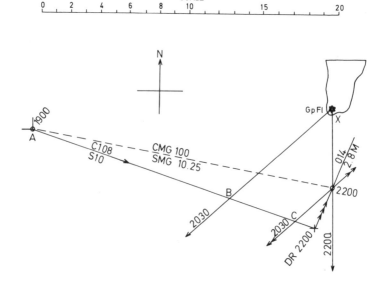

The two LOP's are plotted and the course line from 1900.
The intersection of the course line and the LOP is labelled B.
Point C is marked on the course line such that the ratio of distances is:

$$\frac{\text{distance AB}}{\text{distance BC}} = \frac{\text{time interval between fix and first LOP}}{\text{time interval between first and second LOP's}}$$

in this case:

$$\frac{14}{\text{BC}} = \frac{1.5}{0.5} \quad \text{therefore:} \quad \text{BC} = 4.6 \text{ miles}$$

The first LOP is transferred through C.
The fix is the intersection of the two LOP's.
The DR for 2200 is plotted and the set and drift will be the vector from the DR to the fix.
The course and speed made good from 1900 may be obtained and the intended track may be plotted from the fix.
Note: The course line AC could have been plotted in any direction and provided the ratio AB/BC is maintained, the same fix will result. However, the value of the set and drift would not be the same.

RUNNING FIX WITH COURSE ALTERATION

Worked Example

At 2200 the light K was observed to bear 045°T. Course 105°T at 14 knots.
    At 2245 course was altered to 165°T and at 2315 the light L was observed to bear 127°T.
    The current was estimated to set 244° at 3.5 knots.
    Plot the position of the ship at 2315.

The fact that two different objects were used and a course alteration occurred does not affect the procedure for obtaining the fix.
    Any point may be selected on the first LOP and the intended track plotted from 2200 to 2245.
    The new intended track will be plotted from the end of the first run, i.e. 2245 to 2315, the time of the last bearing.
    The first LOP will be transferred to this point and where it intersects the second LOP is the fix for 2315.
    The intended track will be plotted from this point.

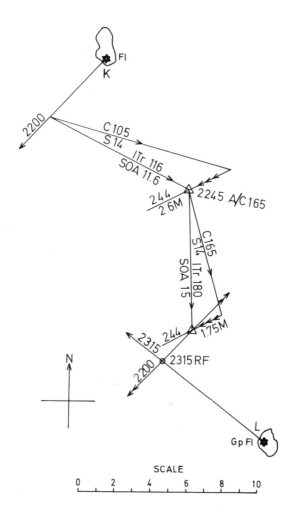

DOUBLING THE ANGLE ON THE BOW

This is simply a particular case of the running fix but using relative bearings instead of compass bearings. If the relative bearing of a particular object is observed, the distance run between the time of observation and the time when the relative bearing is doubled is equal to the distance off the object at the time of the second observation, provided the vessel is not subjected to leeway or current effect.

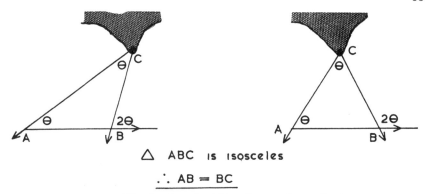

△ ABC is isosceles

∴ AB = BC

Diagram illustrating doubling the angle on the bow.

Note: usually the relative angle θ is less than 45° but this is not essential.

THE FOUR POINT BEARING

A further refinement of the running fix and also of 'doubling the angle on the bow' whereby the initial angle is 45°, or four points, on the bow and the last bearing is 90° on the bow, or abeam.

The effects of current and leeway are incorporated in this problem but as with all types of 'running fix', inaccuracy in the prediction of course and distance made good by the vessel will result in error in the final position.

Worked Example

A vessel is steering 326°C, error 7°E. A light is observed four points on the starboard bow and after steaming for one hour at 14 knots the light was observed abeam. Wind NE and leeway estimated at 7°, current setting 200° at 3 knots. Find the distance off the light at the time of the beam bearing.

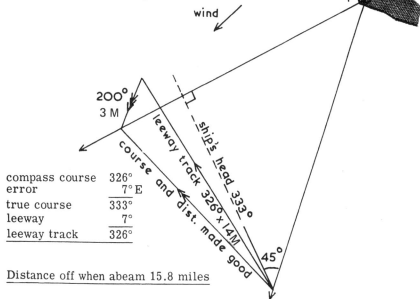

compass course	326°
error	7° E
true course	333°
leeway	7°
leeway track	326°

Distance off when abeam 15.8 miles

DIFFERENCE IN COTANGENTS

Another particular case of the running fix is illustrated with the method known as 'the difference of cotangents'.

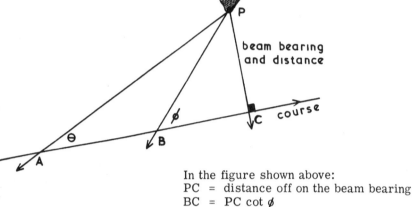

In the figure shown above:

PC = distance off on the beam bearing
BC = $PC \cot \phi$
AC = $PC \cot \theta$

$$AB = (AC - BC) = PC \cot \theta - PC \cot \phi$$
$$= PC(\cot \theta - \cot \phi)$$

therefore AB = PC when $(\cot \theta - \cot \phi) = 1$

i.e. the distance run between bearings will be equal to the distance off on the beam bearing when the difference between the cotangents of the first and second bearings is unity.

TRANSFERRING THE CIRCLE OF POSITION

Not all position lines from terrestrial objects are straight lines and it is sometimes necessary to transfer a circle of position in order to obtain a fix. This would, in fact, be a running fix using a curved position line.

Since it is impossible to transfer a curve in the same manner that a straight line is transferred, see page 46, the only solution to this problem is to transfer the centre of the circle, thereby transferring the whole circle.

Worked Example

A light (height 121 feet) is observed to rise and two hours later it is observed to dip. In the interval the vessel steered 200°T at 11 knots, current setting 326°T. at 2 knots. Height of eye of the observer 49 feet. Plot the position of the vessel at the time of rising and dipping.

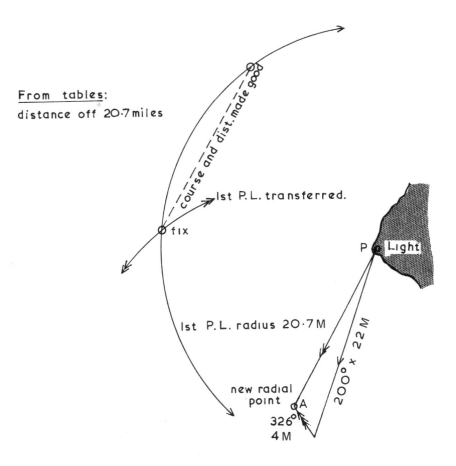

From tables:

distance off 20·7 miles

course and dist. made good

1st P.L. transferred.

fix

P Light

1st P.L. radius 20·7M

200° x 22 M

new radial point A

326° 4 M

The true course of the vessel is laid off from the light P, together with the set and drift (326° x 4 miles). The position A thus obtained is the transfer of the radial point for the position circle. The intersection of the transferred circle of position with the original position line is the fix at the time the light dipped. By running the course made good back from this fix the position at the time the light rose is obtained.

RUNNING FIX WITH A CURVED POSITION LINE

Worked Example

At 1345, by means of a vertical sextant angle, the distance off light 0 is 6.5 miles. The course is 100°T and speed 12 knots. The current is estimated to set 200° at 3 knots. At 1445 the light P bore 030°T.
Plot the fix at the time of the last bearing.

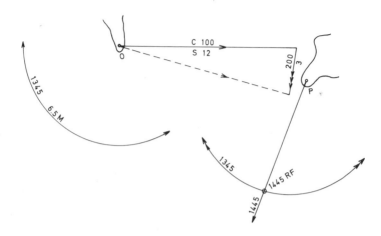

The distance off the light is plotted as a curved LOP as shown in the diagram. The second LOP is also plotted. The only way to transfer a curved LOP is to move the radial point by the intended track and time interval. The first LOP is then replotted from the new centre and the intersection with the second LOP is the fix.

FIX BY CROSS BEARINGS

The navigator, before taking bearings for position plotting, should select objects that are both conspicuous and marked on the chart. It is good practice to note down the names of the objects and to write the bearings alongside as they are taken. The time of the fix will be the'time of the last bearing.

Where only two objects are selected, the angle of cut should be as near 90° as possible as the effect of any errors in taking the bearings or in laying them off on the chart will be at a minimum. The smaller the angle of cut the greater the effect of any errors as shown in the diagram below.

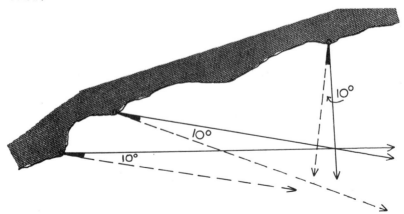

Diagram showing the effect of a 10° error at various angles of cut.

An angle of cut of less than 30° should be rejected if other bearings are available, otherwise the position should be treated with reserve. A good arrangement is to take the first bearing of an object nearly ahead (slow rate of change of bearing) and the second bearing of an object abeam (faster rate of change of bearing).

Where three objects are used it is best if the angle of cut is as near 60° as possible but on no account should the three objects and the observer lie on the circumference of a common circle.

Always select objects near the ship since long lines of bearings drawn on a chart are more susceptible to distortion than shorter lines, and any error in the bearing of a nearby object will have less effect on the accuracy of the final position than a similar error in the bearing of a distant object. The first bearing should be of the most distant object and the last bearing of the object closest to the ship.

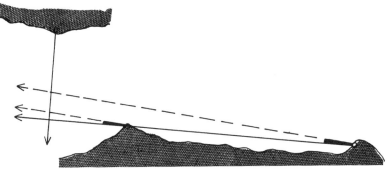

Diagram showing the effect of a 5° error in bearings
of close and distant objects.

When the vessel is in an area where the coastlines were surveyed at different dates, as in the Gulf of Suez, all selected objects for bearings should be on the one coastline.

If three bearings are taken of close objects from a moving ship it is unlikely that they will intersect at a common point and they will, in fact, form a triangle known as the 'cocked hat'.

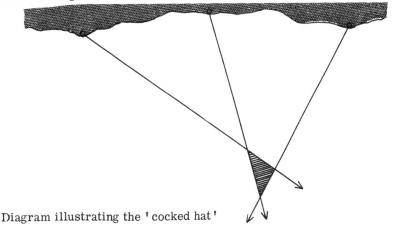

Diagram illustrating the 'cocked hat'

To overcome this it is necessary to transfer the first and second bearings by amounts equal to the course and distance made good by the vessel in the intervals between bearings.

Worked Example

A vessel is steering 100° T. at a speed of 15 knots and obtains the following bearings:

      at 1100 hours Point A bearing 243° T.
      at 1103 hours Beacon B bearing 328° T.
      at 1107 hours Lighthouse C bearing 015° T.

Plot the position of the ship at the time of the last bearing.

Note: the time interval between bearings is somewhat larger than an experienced observer would allow, but it is used here for clarity of explanation.

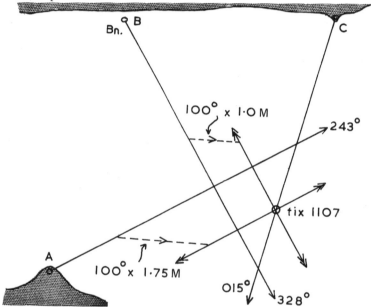

If, after the transfer of the first two bearings, a large 'cocked hat' still exists, it may be due to one or more of the following:

    1. wrong identification of the object,
    2. error in plotting the bearings,
    3. unknown compass error,
    4. compass error wrongly applied,
    5. poor survey of the area.

Numbers 1 and 2 can be eliminated by careful checking and if necessary, taking fresh bearings. Number 3 should be forestalled by checking the compass error at every opportunity by:

    a. transits
    b. by amplitude or time azimuth as explained in any work on celestial navigation,
    c. by station pointer fix

Number 4 error can be removed by re-checking the working and error 5 can only be judged as described in the section on Nautical Charts.

If the 'cocked hat' cannot be reduced by any of the above methods, the position of the ship should be taken as that part of the 'cocked hat' which will place the ship closest to danger.

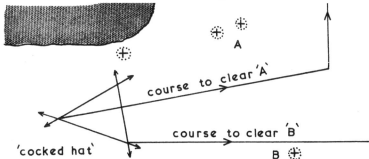

The above diagram shows that the part of the 'cocked hat' closest to immediate danger is not necessarily the one to use, but consideration should be made of the vessel's intended movements.

FIX BY A SINGLE BEARING AND HORIZONTAL ANGLE

Due to the location of the compass it may be possible to take the bearing of one object while a second selected object is screened from the compass position. The sextant angle subtended by the two objects should be observed. The fix can then be obtained by:

1. applying the horizontal angle to the true bearing of the first object thus obtaining the true bearing of the second. The fix being laid off as cross bearings;

2. laying off the first bearing and from any point on this line lay off the horizontal angle using one edge of the parallel ruler. Then transfer this line with the ruler as shown in the diagram below.

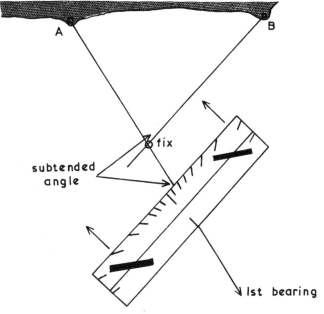

70

FIX BY MEANS OF A TRANSIT AND AN ANGLE

This is the same method as the previous one, except that the observer
uses a transit instead of a compass bearing.

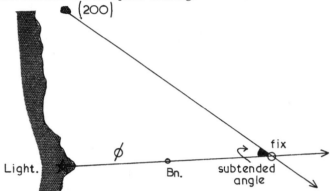

The obvious advantage is that there cannot be any inaccuracy from an
unknown compass error but it is limited due to the necessity of finding
reasonable transits.

FIX BY A BEARING AND A SOUNDING

A compass bearing and a corrected sounding will fix the ship's position
within certain limitations provided it is remembered that:

1. allowance must be made for the height of the tide in order to reduce
    the sounding to chart datum,
2. the angle of cut between the bearing and the fathom contour must be
    as near 90° as possible,
3. the fix will not be reliable unless the fathom contours are clearly
    defined,
4. the bearing should only cross the particular fathom contour in one
    position otherwise doubt will exist as to the vessel's true position.

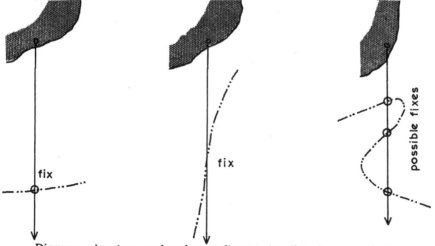

Diagram showing good and poor fixes using the above method.

BEARING AND A SMALL HORIZONTAL ANGLE

This method of obtaining a fix is useful when the only available objects for bearings are extremely close together or when passing a small island. If normal bearings are taken the angle of cut will be too small to produce a reasonable fix.

In this case the horizontal angle between the two objects or the edges of the island is measured and at the same time a bearing is taken of one of the objects. From the charted distance between the two points the distance off may be found as shown:

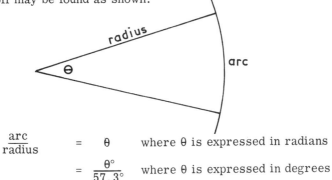

$$\frac{arc}{radius} = \theta \qquad \text{where } \theta \text{ is expressed in radians}$$

$$= \frac{\theta°}{57.3°} \qquad \text{where } \theta \text{ is expressed in degrees}$$

re-arranging: $\quad radius = \dfrac{arc \times 57.3°}{\theta°}$

therefore: distance off $= \dfrac{\text{charted distance} \times 57.3°}{\text{horizontal angle}}$

Worked Example

An observer notes that the charted beacons A and B subtend a horizontal angle of 9° and at the same time the bearing of A is 073°T. The distance between A and B, from the chart, is found to be 2.6 miles. Plot the position of the observer.

$$\text{distance off} = \frac{2.6 \times 57.3°}{9°}$$

$$= 16.6 \text{ miles}$$

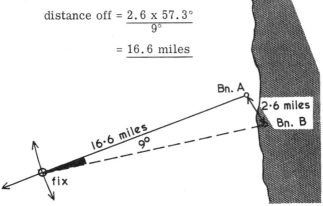

Note: this method only produces reasonable answers when the two objects are virtually equidistant from the observer and the horizontal angle must be small, say not more than 15°.

FIXING THE POSITION BY BEARING AND DISTANCE

This method is normally used when there is only one object available and the position is found by a bearing and the distance off the object, the latter being determined by several methods:

  a. a radar range
  b. a dipping distance
  c. a vertical sextant angle

Worked Example

Point A is observed to bear 216° T. and the distance off by radar is 12 miles. Plot the vessel's position.

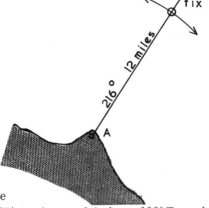

Worked Example

The lighthouse (P) is observed to bear 100° T. and the vertical sextant angle subtended by the lighthouse is 00° 36'.5, plot the position of the vessel.

From Burton's Tables (Table 35):
distance off = 3.25 miles.

Fl. ev. 5 sec. 210 ft. 21M

Worked Example

The lighthouse (P) is observed to dip below the horizon while bearing 265° T. Height of eye of the observer 36'. Plot the position of the vessel.

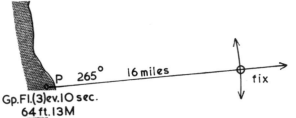

Gp.Fl.(3)ev.10 sec.
64 ft.13M

$1.15\sqrt{36}$ = 6.9 miles
$1.15\sqrt{64}$ = 9.2 miles
distance = 16.1 miles

FIXING BY MEANS OF A LINE OF SOUNDINGS

When no objects are available for the more normal methods of fixing as may occur in conditions of restricted visibility or with poorly marked low lying coastlines, the position of the ship may be ascertained by a succession of soundings. The position is not a fix in the true sense of the word, i.e. an intersection of two or more position lines, but simply an indication of the vessel's whereabouts.

A series of soundings is taken and should be corrected for the height of the tide; if possible, samples of the bottom of the sea-bed would be an asset. The resultant soundings are then compared with the charted depths in order to obtain the ship's position.

PROCEDURE

Mark the corrected soundings on a piece of paper, each sounding separated by the charted distance made good in the time interval. The paper is then moved over the chart parallel to the course made good until the soundings match with the charted depths. It may be more convenient to use a piece of tracing paper marked with meridians to facilitate its movement on the chart parallel to the course made good. An even easier method would be to mark the edge of the parallel rules as indicated, the rules are then set to the track and moved until the soundings agree.

Worked Example

The following corrected soundings were obtained while the vessel was steering 075°T, speed 12 knots and the current was known to be setting 310°T. at 2 knots; 1000 - 15 fms. 1010 - 18 fms. 1015 - 20 fms. 1022 - 20 fms. 1030 - 26 fms. 1040 - 35 fms. 1045 - 40 fms. Plot the position of the ship at 1045.

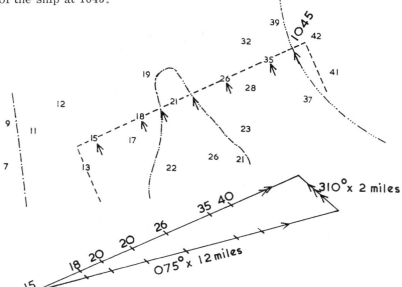

To facilitate the plotting of the distance made good between each sounding it is easier to plot the course steered on the chart and this is marked off in the sounding intervals. Parallel lines to the set, if any, drawn through the points on the course line will intersect the track at the appropriate intervals as shown in this and the following example.

Worked Example

A vessel is steering 093° T. speed 15 knots. The current is setting 176°T. at 3 knots. The following soundings (corrected) were obtained:
0600 - 23 fms.   0612 - 30 fms.   0618 - 33 fms.   0630 - 42 fms.   0635 - 36 fms.   0641 - 30 fms.   0650 - 24 fms.   Plot the vessel's position at 0650.

Note: Unless the soundings show some marked degree of change it may be possible to fit the line of soundings in several positions on the chart. Even under ideal conditions the position obtained by this method should be treated with caution and the position checked by other means as soon as possible.

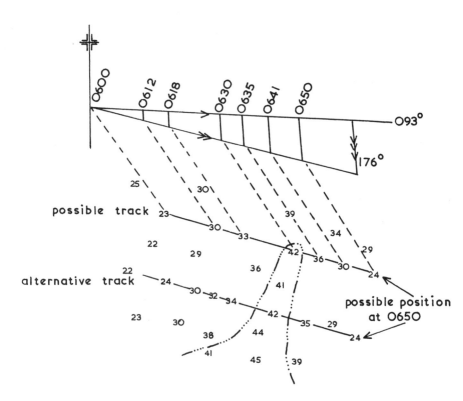

FIXING WITH HORIZONTAL SEXTANT ANGLES

On page 41 the method of obtaining a position line by means of a horizontal sextant angle is described in detail. If two of these position lines are obtained simultaneously their point of intersection will be the ship's position at the time of observation.

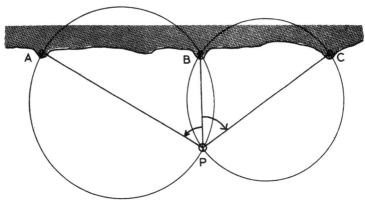

In the diagram above, A and B are two objects on the shore in the same plane as the observer. If the horizontal angle between them is observed the vessel will lie on the arc APB that bounds the segment containing the observed angle. If the angle between B and C is observed the vessel will lie on the arc BPC which bounds the segment containing the second observed angle. The arcs will intersect at B and P, the latter being the position of the ship.

Advantages: 1. it is independent of compass error,
                   2. the angles may be observed from any part of the ship,
                   3. an extremely accurate fix can be obtained since the sextant can be read more accurately than a compass,
                   4. the horizontal angles can be observed by compass (the horizontal angles will be the angles contained by the compass bearings) or by sextant.

Disadvantages: 1. three suitable objects are necessary,
                      2. if the selected objects are incorrectly identified or charted the error in the resultant position may not be apparent. When in doubt fix by cross bearings,
                      3. the time taken to plot is considerably longer than any other method.

    If the three objects together with the observer lie on the arc of a common circle, the observer can be anywhere on the seaward arc of this circle and consequently the fix is unreliable. This will also occur with cross bearings if the above condition is fulfilled and the compass error is in any doubt.

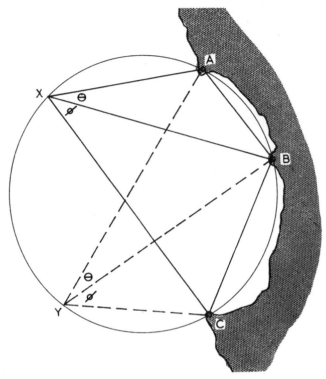

In the diagram above, points A, B and C lie on the arc of a circle that also passes through X and Y. The angle subtended by the chord AB (θ) is constant over the major segment AXYCB; similarly, the angle subtended by the chord BC (ϕ) is constant over the major segment BAXYC. The arc AXYC is common to both major segments and consequently the observer may be situated anywhere on this arc.

To eliminate this occurrence the objects should be selected so that:

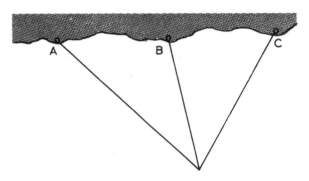

1. they are on, or near the same straight line as shown above.

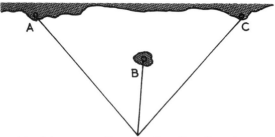

2. the centre object is nearer the ship than the other two as shown above.
3. the observer lies inside the triangle formed by the objects as shown
   below.

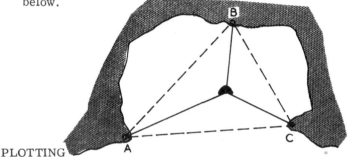

PLOTTING

There are four methods of plotting the fix from horizontal sextant angles:

1. by geometrical construction,
2. by station pointer,
3. using tracing paper as a station pointer,
4. using the Douglas Protractor, this latter instrument is seen more
   amongst yachtsmen than among professional navigators yet it has
   much to recommend it for chartwork.

GEOMETRICAL CONSTRUCTION

The charted positions of the first two objects are joined by a straight
line. This is a chord of the required position circle. If the observed
angle is less than 90° the vessel lies on a major segment, i.e. the
vessel and the centre of the position circle are on the same side of the
chord. If the observed angle is greater than 90° the vessel lies on a
minor segment, i.e. the centre of the position circle and the vessel are
on opposite sides of the chord.

The centre of the position circle is found by constructing an isosceles
triangle with the chord as base. The equal base angles of this triangle
are found as follows:

if the observed angle is less than 90° then (90° - obs.angle) is laid
from each point towards the observer,
if the observed angle is greater than 90° then (obs.angle - 90°) is
laid from each point away from the observer.

The position circle is constructed with the apex of the isosceles triangle as centre and radius to either of the observed points. The process
is repeated with the second observation.

78

Worked Example

The following horizontal angles were obtained simultaneously: A to B
67° and B to C 104°. Plot the position of the observer.
Note: the observed angles would normally be written: A 67° B 104° C.

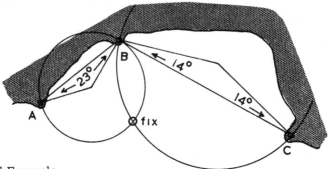

Worked Example

The following compass bearings were taken: A bore 321° C. B bore
014° C. C bore 072° C. Plot the position of the ship and determine the
error of the compass for the ship's head.

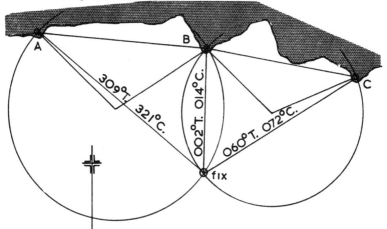

321° to 014° = 53° horizontal angle.
therefore angles laid off from A and B seawards = 90° - 53° = 37°
014° to 072° = 58° horizontal angle.
therefore angles laid off from B and C seawards = 90° - 58° = 32°

After the position has been plotted, either geometrically or by station
pointer, the bearings are marked in and compared with the true meridian
or compass rose.

true bearing of A   = 309°...of B = 002°...of C = 060°
compass bearing of A = 321°...of B = 014°...of C = 072°

compass error   12° W.   12° W.   12° W.

While theoretically the compass error must be the same for each bearing
since the ship's head is constant, it is advisable to check each bearing
and to take the mean error.

PLOTTING WITH THE STATION POINTER

As shown in the diagram below, the station pointer consists of a graduated disc from which radiate three 'legs', the centre one being fixed and the outer pair, termed 'left' and 'right' being moveable and can be clamped to any position on the graduated disc. The working edges of the three legs are bevelled and are extensions of radii of the graduated disc. The centre of the latter is indicated by a 'v' cut in the centre leg or by a small hole.

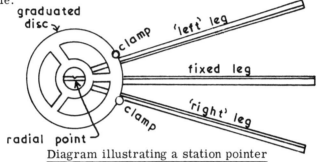

Diagram illustrating a station pointer

When using the station pointer the 'left' leg is set to the angle between the centre object and that object lying to the observer's left hand. The 'right' leg is similarly set to the angle between the centre object and the object to the observer's right hand. The station pointer is then moved on the chart until the three bevelled edges coincide with the observed objects, the 'centre' leg coincident with the centre object. The position of the ship is marked with a sharp pencil at the centre of the graduated disc.

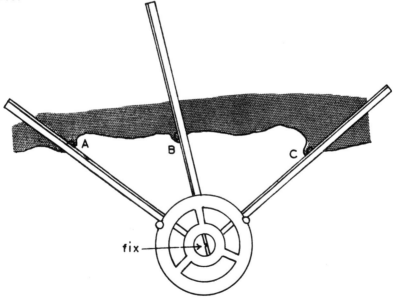

Diagram illustrating plotting with the station pointer

The bevelled edge of the 'right' leg cannot be brought close to the 'centre' leg and cannot, therefore, be used for small angles. When the 'right' angle is small it should be set between the 'centre' leg and the 'left' leg; the 'right' leg is then moved round and set to the sum of the two angles, measured from the fixed leg. When in position on the chart the fixed leg will be coincident with the right hand object.

When the observer is equipped with a station pointer it is good practice when taking the horizontal angles to observe a 'check' angle between the centre object and a fourth object. When the station pointer is in position and held steady, one of the legs is moved to the check angle and its bevelled edge should then be coincident with the fourth object.

PLOTTING WITH TRACING PAPER

The horizontal angles are plotted on tracing paper as shown. The lines AO, BO and CO represent the legs of the station pointer and are moved on the chart until they are coincident with the observed objects. The position of the ship at O is simply pricked through to the surface of the chart.

<u>Using tracing paper as a station pointer</u>

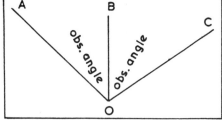

PLOTTING WITH THE DOUGLAS PROTRACTOR

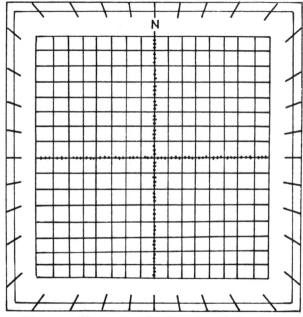

<u>Diagram illustrating the Douglas protractor</u>

This instrument has a number of uses and consists of a transparent plastic square protractor manufactured in a number of sizes up to 10" square. It is marked with a square lattice and the edge is graduated in degrees from 0° to 359° both clockwise and anti-clockwise. The under side is matt enabling pencil lines to be drawn and at the centre is a small hole large enough to take the point of a sharp pencil.

USE AS A STATION POINTER

The horizontal angles are laid off on the matt side on either side of the N.S. line and radiating from the centre. The protractor is then moved on the chart until the lines are coincident with the charted objects. The position of the ship is marked with a pencil through the centre hole.
Note: since the matt underside is used the angles must be reversed left for right and right for left.

OTHER USES OF THE DOUGLAS PROTRACTOR

1. Laying off Courses or Bearings.
The centre hole and the required course or bearing must be aligned with any convenient meridian. The protractor is then moved along the meridian until the left or right hand edge passes through the point from which the course is to be laid off, or through which the bearing is to be drawn.

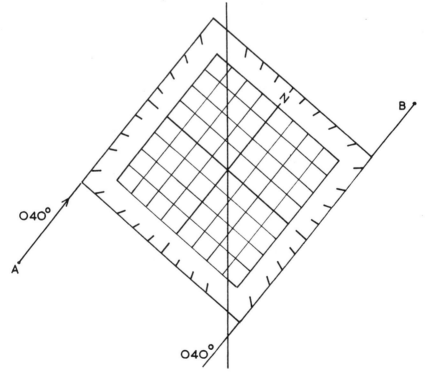

In the simplified diagram above the Douglas Protractor is used to lay off a course of 040° from A. Note that the right hand edge could be used to lay off a bearing of B as 040°.

2. To read off Courses or Bearings

The left or right hand edge, or one of the lines of the lattice parallel to these edges, is placed along the course or bearing so that the centre hole is on a meridian. Where the meridian cuts the edge of the protractor the figure on the inner scale gives the course or bearing.

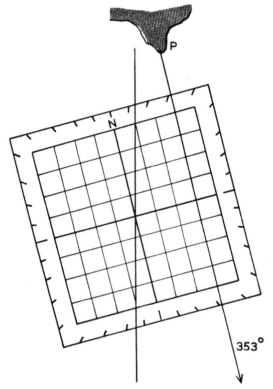

3. Parallel Rules

The protractor is set up with one of the parallel lattice lines on the bearing or course and by drawing pencil lines along the edge parallel to the lattice the bearing/course can be transferred to the point required without displacement.

4. To obtain the Compass Error

The compass bearings of three objects are marked on the matt side of the protractor which is then used as a station pointer and the ship's position plotted. The protractor is then checked against the meridian and the amount by which the zero is displaced from the true north of the chart is the compass error. This can also be effected against the compass rose.

5. To find the Position from a Line of Soundings

The corrected soundings are marked on the edge of the protractor at the appropriate intervals instead of on paper.

TO FIND THE COURSE MADE GOOD FROM THREE BEARINGS OF ONE OBJECT

This is not a method of fixing the ship but simply enables the navigator to determine the course made good by the ship. It is often referred to as the 'three bearing problem'.

In order that the correct results are obtained it is important that:
1. the vessel maintains her course and speed through the water,
2. the tidal stream, if any, is constant throughout.

The solution of the 'three bearing problem' is based on the geometry of the proportional division of straight lines.

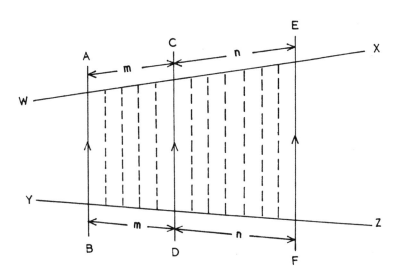

Given: AB, CD and EF are three straight parallel lines.
WX and YZ are straight but not necessarily parallel lines.
To prove:

BD:DF = AC:CE.

Proof:
Assume that BD:DF = m:n

i.e. if BD is divided into 'm' equal parts, then DF may be divided into 'n' such equal parts.

If lines parallel to AB are drawn through the points of division in BD and DF they will divide the segments AC and CE into parts which are all equal, of which AC contains 'm' and CE contains 'n'.

Therefore: AC:CE = m:n
and: AC:CE = BD:DF

If three successive bearings are taken of the point A then three position lines AX, AY and AZ are obtained as shown in the figure below. If the distance steamed between the first and second bearings is 'x' miles and the distance between the second and third bearings is 'y' miles, then the course made good is found by using the principle previously explained.

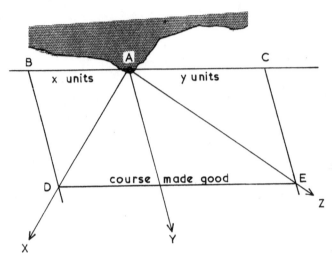

A 'ratio line' is drawn through A in any direction. AB and AC are marked off, using any convenient units, in the ratio of the distances steamed, i.e. AB = x units and AC = y units. Parallel lines to the central position line AY are drawn from B and C to intersect the first and third position lines at D and E respectively. If D and E are joined this line gives the direction made good in the period between the first and third bearings, irrespective of the tidal stream that may be running.

Note: It is most important to remember that only the course made good can be found. In order to fix the position of the ship and hence obtain the actual track, additional information must be given.

It is not necessary to know the distances steamed as the time interval between the bearings may be used, since the time taken will be a function of the distance steamed.

In the above example the ratio line would be divided into the ratio of the time intervals, i.e. time between first and second bearings is 'm' minutes and the time taken between second and third bearings is 'n' minutes then the ratio AB:AC = m:n, again any convenient units may be used.

This technique would only be used if it is impossible to obtain a fix from A or surrounding objects.

Worked Example

A vessel steering 082°T. observes the following bearings of P. At 1015 - 046°T. At 1030 - 012°T. At 1055 - 325°T. The current is known to be setting 174°T. at 4 knots. Plot the position of the ship at the time of the last bearing and find the vessel's speed.

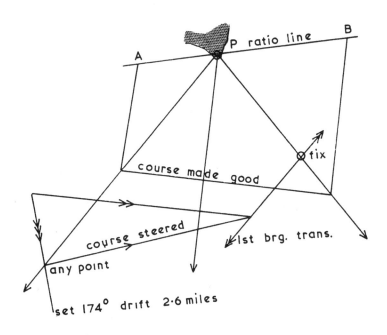

Note: Since there is no information as to the speed of the vessel it is necessary to use the time ratio to subdivide the ratio line.

$$\text{i.e. } \frac{AP}{PB} = \frac{15}{25} = \frac{3}{5}$$

$$\text{Set } = 174°$$
$$\text{Drift } = \frac{4 \times 40}{60} = 2.6 \text{ miles}$$

Speed of vessel 12 knots

Worked Example

A vessel is steering 076° C. from a fix obtained at 1400 (position A). At 1500 point P bore 60° on the port bow and at 1530 the point was abeam. Compass error 9° E. Current unknown. Speed of vessel 14 knots. Plot the position of the ship at the time of the last bearing and find the set and drift experienced since 1400.

Compass course	076°	
Error	9° E.	
True course	085°	
	60°	angle on port bow
	025° T.	1st bearing
True course	085°	
	90°	
	355° T.	beam bearing.

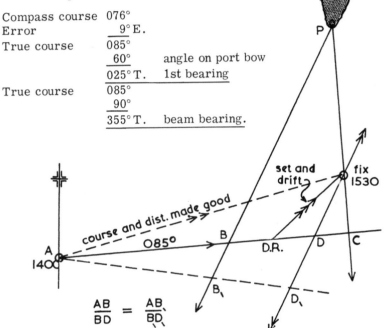

Construction:

Lay off the two bearings from P and also the true course from A. Let this course intersect the 1st and 2nd bearings at B and C respectively.
Construct BD

such that: $\dfrac{AB}{BD} = \dfrac{\text{time or distance, if known, between fix and B}}{\text{time or distance, if known, between B and C}}$

$\qquad = \dfrac{60}{30} = \dfrac{2}{1}$

Transfer 1st position line through D, the intersection of the transferred position line and the second bearing is the fix at 1530. In order to find the set and drift it is necessary to plot the D.R. position for 1530. The line joining the D.R. and the fix at 1530 is the set and drift experienced since 1400.

Note: The course line AC could have been drawn in any direction and provided the ratio of $\dfrac{AB}{BD}$ is maintained, the same fix will result but not the set and drift.

TO FIND THE POSITION AND COURSE AND DISTANCE MADE GOOD
BY MEANS OF THREE BEARINGS — NOT OF THE SAME OBJECT

Note: In this case two bearings are taken of one object and one bearing
is taken of another object. The course steered is known as is the
direction of the current. The time between bearings is also known.

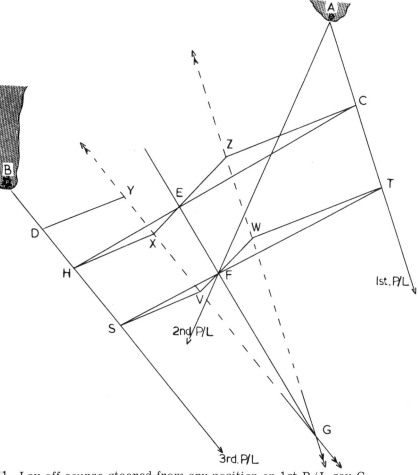

1. Lay off course steered from any position on 1st P/L say C.
2. Mark run between 1st and 2nd P/L's (CZ) from 1st P/L and between
   2nd and 3rd P/L's (DY) backwards from 3rd P/L.
3. Transfer 1st and 3rd P/L's through Z and Y to cut at G.
4. Draw in current between 1st and 3rd transferred P/L's (ZX).
5. Draw XH parallel to DY.
6. Join CH and call point where this cuts current E.
     Note: CH is not course made good .
7. Join GE. The point F where GE cuts the middle bearing is the fix.
8. Draw the current through F cutting 1st and 3rd transferred P/L's at
   W and V. Draw WT and VS parallel to ZC and YD. Join TS to get
   the course and distance made good. WV is the drift.

6
TIDES

I N ORDER to understand the basic causes of the tide raising forces it is necessary to consider the Earth and Moon as an independent planetary system. These two bodies rotate around a common centre of gravity known as the 'barycentre' which lies on a line joining their physical centres.

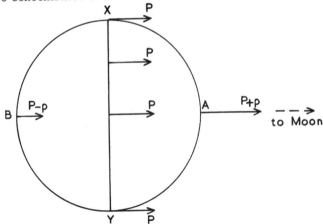

The rotation of the bodies follows the laws governing circular motion, one of which states that this motion will occur when a body moving at constant speed is acted upon by a constant force perpendicular to the direction of motion. This constant force is the gravitational attraction of the Earth for the Moon and vice-versa. Equilibrium is achieved in this system so that the orbital speed of the Moon is not sufficient to carry it out into space or small enough to allow a collision between Moon and Earth.

In considering the effects of the inter-body gravitational attraction it must be remembered that the Earth is a dense rigid body whose mass acts at its centre of gravity, also the oceans - relatively dense but non-rigid - are concentrated on the surface of the Earth.

In the figure the points A and B are on the diameter joining the centres of the Earth and Moon. X and Y lie on the meridian that is perpendicular to the line of centres and for all practical purposes may be considered to be equidistant with the centre of the Earth from the centre of the Moon. If the force of the Moon's attraction at the centre of the Earth is represented by P, then at all points on the meridian XY the force will have this same constant value. At position A there will be an increase in this force (P + p) which will be a maximum value at the minimum distance from the Moon. At position B the force becomes (P-p) the minimum value at the maximum distance from the Moon.

Thus at A, the force on the Earth is P and on the water (P + p) which results in a differential force on the water of + p causing a piling up of the water under the Moon.

At B, the force on the Earth is P and on the water (P - p), here the differential force of - p is pulling the Earth away from the water which results in a tendency for the water to be left behind. The differential force at the meridian XY will be zero.

The Earth rotates, relative to the Moon, once in a lunar day of approximately 24 hours and 50 minutes, so that at any point on the Earth's surface this differential attraction, or tide raising force, will follow a simple cosine curve, as shown in the figure, having two complete cycles each lunar day.

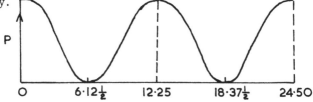

These forces produce two equal maximum and minimum tides per lunar day and are termed semi-diurnal (one cycle each half day). This will occur at all places only when the declination of the Moon is 0°.

The effect of a change in the declination of the Moon is to produce variations in the maximum and minimum tide raising forces, also in the times between successive maxima and minima.

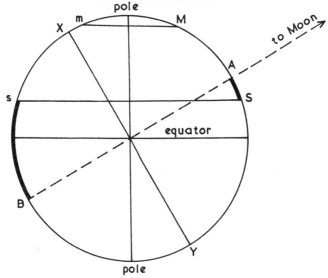

In the figure, A and B are the extremes of the diameter of the Earth on the line joining the centres of the Earth and Moon. In this case the Moon has northerly declination. X and Y are on the meridian whose plane is perpendicular to diameter AB, consequently the tide raising forces on this meridian are zero. On the parallel of latitude Mm the maximum force occurs at 'M' and the minimum force at 'm', but at no time does this force reach zero value. The forces now have only one maxima and one minima as shown, which produces a diurnal tide (one tidal cycle per lunar day).

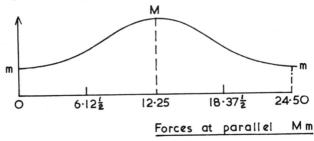

Forces at parallel   M m

On the parallel Ss the maximum forces occur at 'S' and 's' which are different distances from A and B where the greatest forces exist, this results in alternate maxima of different height and unequal intervals between successive maxima and minima as shown. This diurnal inequality is commonly found in the tides as they actually exist.

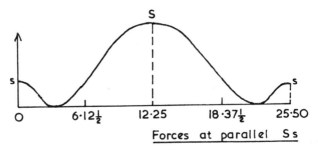

Forces at parallel   S s

The effect of the Sun is also to generate a differential attraction which also results in tide generating forces, these being superimposed on the forces of the Moon.

The combined diurnal and semi-diurnal tide raising forces set up small oscillations in the large oceanic basins, probably not more than two feet in amplitude, but as these oscillations approach shallow water the amplitude and form is radically changed in the same way that an ocean swell acquires a steep front as it approaches the shore. Under certain geographical circumstances, such as the Severn estuary which gradually shelves and concentrates the wave form with its narrowing entrance, the amplitude can be increased to twenty feet or more.

TIDAL DATUMS

The following diagram illustrates the various tidal levels used in navigation.

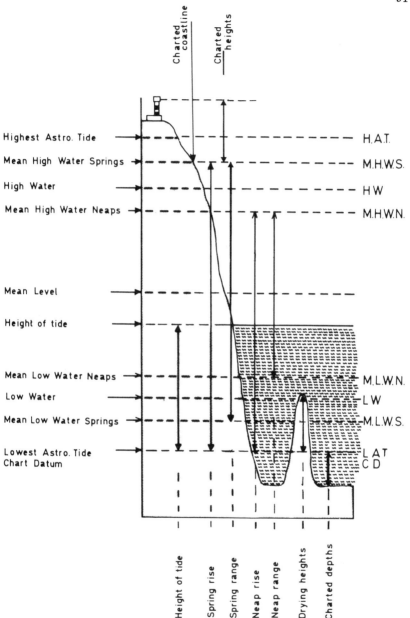

H.A.T. *(Highest astronomical tide)*
L.A.T. *(Lowest astronomical tide)*
These are the highest and lowest levels which can be predicted to occur under average meteorological conditions and under any combination of astronomical conditions. These levels will not necessarily be reached every year.

M.H.W.S. (Mean high water springs)
M.L.W.S. (Mean low water springs)
This is the average, throughout the year when the average maximum declination of the moon is $23\frac{1}{2}°$, of the heights of two successive high and low waters during those periods of 24 hours (approximately every two weeks) when the range of the tide is greatest.

M.H.W.N. (Mean high water neaps)
M.L.W.N. (Mean low water neaps)
The definition in these cases is the same as for Spring Tides except that the average is taken when the range of the tide is least.

It should be noted that the above levels will vary from year to year over a period of approximately 18.61 years when the line of nodes or orbital intersections return to the same position with respect to the sun, earth and moon.

M.S.L. (Mean sea level)
This is the average level of the sea over the period of approximately 18.61 years, or the average level that would exist in the absence of tides.

Occasionally certain Tide Tables will refer to Higher High Water (H.H.W.) and to Lower Low Water (L.L.W.). This refers to positions where the tide is semidiurnal and would be the higher of the two successive high tides and the lower of the two successive low tides.

TIDE TABLES AND THE TIDAL PROBLEM FOR THE NAVIGATOR

Most maritime nations produce their own Tide Tables which are based on information exchanged between nations conducting tidal observations and predictions.

In all cases daily predictions are given for STANDARD or REFERENCE positions (usually major ports) with additional information being provided to enable the navigator to predict the tide at SECONDARY or SUBORDINATE positions.

These secondary positions are based on a particular standard position where the tidal characteristics are most like those of the secondary position. This is why it may seem strange to the navigator to find secondary positions such as the Hudson Strait in Canada based on the reference position of Puerto Gallegos located in Argentina.

In general, the tidal problem is based on the fact that the rise and fall of the tide closely follows a simple cosine curve. Since this is not completely true, inaccuracies in the results will be inevitable but they are not of significance to the navigator.

USE OF THE ADMIRALTY TIDE TABLES

These tables are divided into three volumes covering the world.

Volume 1, covering European waters is unique in that it provides a prediction curve for all standard ports which considerably improves the accuracy of prediction. In addition a specimen format with instructions is provided.

The key to accuracy in working any tidal problem can be found in the consistent use of a logically arranged, well organised form. Once the form is established, the tide problems are easily completed using simple arithmetic.

For the first worked example, the form together with the very explicit instructions are reprinted. For the succeeding problems only the form is printed.

The reader is reminded that the predicted heights given in all tide tables are heights above Chart Datum for that place. Similarly, the solution to a tidal problem will always give the height above Chart Datum.

Worked Example

Determine the height of the tide at Holyhead at 1200 GMT on February 24th.

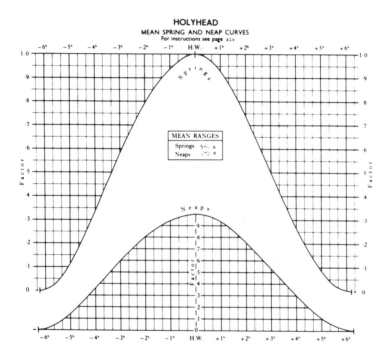

HOLYHEAD
MEAN SPRING AND NEAP CURVES
For instructions see page xiv

WALES - HOLYHEAD

LAT 53°19′N   LONG 4°37′W

TIME ZONE GMT   TIMES AND HEIGHTS OF HIGH AND LOW WATERS   YEAR   1978

FEBRUARY   MARCH

24 0455 0.9   2.8   **22** 0246 1.4   4.7
   1106 5.7 18.6   0857 5.2 16.9
F 1719 0.7   2.4   W 1508 1.1   3.7
   2326 5.5 18.0   2117 5.1 16.9

No.	PLACE	POSITION		TIMES AT STANDARD PORT				HEIGHTS (IN FEET) AT STANDARD PORT			
	STANDARD PORT	Lat. N.	Long. W.	High Water at		Low Water at		MHWS	MHWN	MLWN	MLWS
478	**HOLYHEAD**	(see page 132)		0000 and 1200	0600 and 1800	0500 and 1700	1100 and 2300	**18·6**	**14·7**	**6·5**	**2·3**
479	Porth Ruffydd	53 17	4 40	−0026	−0026	−0021	−0021	−2·3	−1·9	−0·6	−0·2
480	Llanddwyn Island	53 08	4 25	−0053	−0053	−0021	−0021	−4·4	−3·6	−2·3	−0·9
481	Porth Dinllaen	52 56	4 33	−0135	−0105	−0050	−0030	−3·6	−3·4	−0·9	−0·3

INSTRUCTIONS

Box No.

Complete Heading.

1 to 4	Enter daily prediction data from ATT Part I.
5 and 6	Enter data from ATT Part II (not required for Standard Port or Vol. 1).
7 to 10	Enter Differences from ATT Part II (interpolation necessary for Vol 1) (not required for Standard Port).
11	Enter sum of 1 and 7 (for Standard Port enter 1).
12	Enter sum of 2 and 8 (for Standard Port enter 2).
13	Enter sum of 3, 5, 6 and 9 (for Standard Port enter 3).
14	Enter sum of 4, 5, 6 and 10 (for Standard Port enter 4).
15	Enter Duration. Difference of times in 11 and 12 (not required for Vol. 1).
16(a)	Enter Range at Standard Port. Difference of heights in 3 and 4.
16(b)	Enter Range at Secondary Port. Difference of heights in 13 and 14.
	*Delete Springs, Neaps, Interpolate as appropriate to Standard Port Range 16(a) (Vol. 1 only).

TO FIND HEIGHT AT GIVEN TIME

17	Enter required time.
18	Enter HW time from 11.
19	Enter Interval. Difference of 17 and 18.
20	*Enter Factor obtained from interpolation of appropriate curve entered with Interval 19.
21	Enter Rise = Factor 20 × Range 16(b) (for Standard Port use 16(a)).
22	Enter LW Height from 14.
23	Enter sum of Rise 21 and LW Height 22.

TO FIND TIME FOR A GIVEN HEIGHT (Start at bottom of column)

23	Enter required height.
22	Enter LW Height from 14.
21	Enter Rise = Height 23 − LW Height 22.
20	Enter Factor = Rise 21/Range 16(b) (for Standard Ports use 16(a)).
19	*Enter Interval obtained from interpolation of appropriate curve entered with Factor 20.
18	Enter HW Time 11.
17	Enter Interval 19 applied to HW Time 18.

*NOTE Do not attempt to extrapolate additional curves. In ATT Vol. 1 use the Spring curve for Spring Ranges and greater, and the Neap curve for Neap Ranges and less. For intermediate ranges interpolate between curves using the Range at the Standard Port (Box 16(a)) as argument. In ATT Vols. 2 and 3 if duration is outside those shown in Table II use NP 159.

STANDARD PORT **HOLYHEAD** .TIME ~~OR HEIGHT~~ REQUIRED **1200GMT**

SECONDARY PORT.... **—** ...... DATE **24-2-78** .TIME ZONE **0000** .....

	TIME		HEIGHT	
	HW	LW	HW	LW
STANDARD PORT	1 **1106**	2 **1719**	3 **5·7**	4 **0·7**
Seasonal Changes in ML	− Standard Port		5	
	+ Secondary Port		6	
DIFFERENCES	7	8	9	10
SECONDARY PORT	11	12	13	14
DURATION	15 **0613**	RANGE(a)St (b)Sec	16(a) **5·0**	16(b)

*Springs/~~Neaps/Interpolate~~

START – Height at Given Time ↓

REQUIRED TIME	17	**1200**
TIME HW	18	**1106**
INTERVAL	19	**+0054**

FACTOR	20	**0·93**

RISE	21	**4·7**
HEIGHT LW	22	**0·7**
HEIGHT REQUIRED	23	**5·4**

↑ START – Time for Given Height

*Delete as necessary

Worked Example

At what time during the early morning rising tide will there be 3.5 metres above Chart Datum at Holyhead on March 22nd.

STANDARD PORT .**HOLYHEAD**. ~~TIME OR~~ HEIGHT REQUIRED .**3·5**.....

SECONDARY PORT ....**—**...... DATE .**22-3-78**. TIME ZONE .**0000**.....

	TIME		HEIGHT	
	HW	LW	HW	LW
STANDARD PORT	1 **0857**	2 **0246**	3 **5·2**	4 **1·4**
Seasonal Changes in ML	− Standard Port		5	
	+ Secondary Port		6	
DIFFERENCES	7	8	9	10
SECONDARY PORT	11	12	13	14
DURATION	15 **0611**	RANGE(a)St (b)Sec	16(a) **3·8**	16(b)

*~~Springs/Neaps~~/Interpolate

START − Height at Given Time ⤵

REQUIRED TIME	17 **0547**
TIME HW	18 **0857**
INTERVAL	19 **−0310**

SP. − 0310
NP. − 0310

FACTOR	20 **0·55**

RISE	21 **2·1**
HEIGHT LW	22 **1·4**
HEIGHT REQUIRED	23 **3·5**

↑ START Time for Given Height

*Delete as necessary

Worked Example

Determine the height of the tide at 0700 GMT on February 24th at Porth Dinllaen.

STANDARD PORT .HOLYHEAD. TIME ~~OR HEIGHT~~ REQUIRED .0700 GMT.

SECONDARY PORT. PORTH .... DATE 24-2-78 .TIME ZONE 0000 .....
DINLLAEN

	TIME		HEIGHT	
	HW	LW	HW	LW
STANDARD PORT	1 **1106**	2 **0455**	3 **5·7**	4 **0·9**
Seasonal Changes in ML	− Standard Port		5	
	+ Secondary Port		6	
DIFFERENCES	7 **−0130**	8 **−0050**	9 **−1·1**	10 **−0·1**
SECONDARY PORT	11 **0936**	12 **0405**	13 **4·6**	14 **0·8**
DURATION	15 **0531**	RANGE(a)St (b)Sec	16(a) **4·8**	16(b) **3·8**

*Springs/~~Neaps/Interpolate~~

START −
Height at
Given Time

REQUIRED TIME	17	**0700**
TIME HW	18	**0936**
INTERVAL	19	**−0236**

FACTOR	20	**0·67**

RISE	21	**2·6**
HEIGHT LW	22	**0·8**
HEIGHT REQUIRED	23	**3·4**

START −
Time for
Given Height

*Delete as necessary

USE OF THE ADMIRALTY TIDE TABLES OUTSIDE EUROPEAN WATERS

In volumes 2 and 3, individual tidal curves are not published for the various standard ports. At the front of both volumes a curve is published (as shown on the following pages) which is based on a cosine curve. The principle involved is the same as in the previous examples, where a predicted range is multiplied by a factor, the result being added to the height of low water to give the predicted height.

The published curves give the duration of rise or fall in half hour intervals from 5 to 7 hours. For intermediate durations, interpolation must be used but no extrapolation should be attempted.

Should the duration of the tide fall outside the limits of the curves, i.e. less than 5 hours or more than 7 hours, the correct method to use is the Admiralty Method of Tidal Prediction using Harmonic Constants.

Again, it is recommended that the standard format is used as illustrated in the following examples.

TABLE I

FOR FINDING THE HEIGHT OF THE TIDE AT TIMES BETWEEN HIGH AND LOW WATER

HOURLY INTERVAL FROM NEAREST HIGH WATER

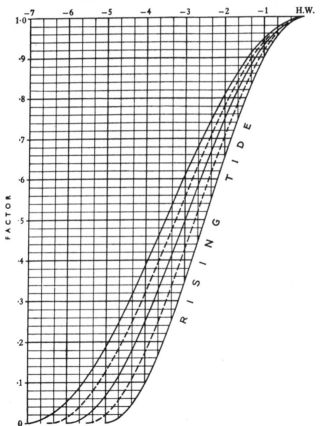

TABLE I

FOR FINDING THE HEIGHT OF THE TIDE AT TIMES BETWEEN HIGH AND LOW WATER

HOURLY INTERVAL FROM NEAREST HIGH WATER

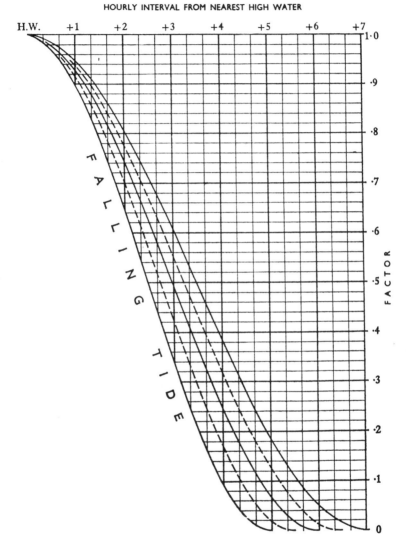

Worked Example

At what time will there be 6.0 metres above Chart Datum at Bhavnagar, West Coast of India on August 16th, 1979 on the morning rising tide.

Year 1979 Extract from Admiralty Tide Tables, Vol. 2.

India, West Coast — Bhavnagar
Lat 21° 45′ N Long 72° 14′ E
Time Zone –0530 Times and heights of high and low water
AUGUST

	0534	2.4
16	1159	9.3
Th	1830	3.3
	0019	8.1
17	0644	2.8
F	1314	9.3
	1954	3.3

No.	Place	Position		Time diff.		Height Diffs. (metres)			
						MHWS	MHWN	MLWN	MLWS
4346	Bhavnagar	21°45′N	72°14′E	MHW	MLW	10.2	8.3	3.5	1.4
4344	Sultanpur	21°17′N	72°08′E	-0100	-0132	–3.3	–2.9	–0.7	–0.4

STANDARD PORT **BHAVNAGAR** TIME OR HEIGHT REQUIRED **6·0**

SECONDARY PORT ... — ... DATE **16-8-79** TIME ZONE **−0530**

	TIME		HEIGHT	
	HW	LW	HW	LW
STANDARD PORT	1 **1159**	2 **0534**	3 **9·3**	4 **2·4**
Seasonal Changes in ML	− Standard Port		5 **NIL**	
	+ Secondary Port		6	
DIFFERENCES	7	8	9	10
SECONDARY PORT	11	12	13	14
DURATION	15 **0625**	RANGE(a)St (b)Sec	16(a) **6·9**	16(b)

*Springs/Neaps/Interpolate

START − Height at Given Time ↓

REQUIRED TIME	17	**0848**
TIME HW	18	**1159**
INTERVAL	19	**− 0310**

FACTOR	20	**0·52**

RISE	21	**3·6**
HEIGHT LW	22	**2·4**
HEIGHT REQUIRED	23	**6·0**

↑ START − Time for Given Height

*Delete as necessary

Enter the times and heights of high and low water for the time period required. Determine the duration, noting whether the tide is rising or falling, and the range of the tide. Starting at the bottom of the form, enter the height required (6.0m), the height of LW (2.4m) and determine the rise of tide required (3.6m). Calculate the factor from:

$$\frac{\text{height above LW}}{\text{range}} = \text{factor}$$

i.e. $\qquad \dfrac{3.6}{6.9} = 0.52$

With this factor and the duration (0625) enter Table 1 on the curves of rising tides. The interval from HW is found to be -0310. This should be entered on the form together with the time of HW and the predicted time obtained.

Worked Example

Determine the height of the tide at Sultanpur at 2100 zone time on the 16th August 1979.

Although Sultanpur is a secondary port the basic principle is the same. Corrections are made to the predictions at the standard port to obtain the secondary port predictions. The predictions for the time period required are entered on the form for Bhavnagar. Any seasonal changes in mean level are entered next. These are found on the lower right hand page of Part II. Note that these are applied algebraically. For example, if the seasonal change for the standard port had been −0.4 it would have been applied as −(−0.4). The time differences for HW and LW are entered and applied to the times at the standard port to give the predicted times at the secondary port. The corresponding height differences are determined next. In the example, the HW height at the standard port is 8.1m and this corresponds to the MHWN value of 8.3m. No interpolation is necessary in this case and the height difference for Sultanpur will be −2.9m. Where the predicted height for the standard port differs from the tabulated values for MHWS, MHWN, MLWN and MLWS interpolation or extrapolation is essential. Having obtained the predicted times and heights for the secondary port, the procedure is the same as in the previous example.

USE OF CANADIAN AND U.S. TIDE TABLES

The Canadian Government publishes Tide Tables covering all Canadian waters, including the Great Lakes. The United States publishes Tide Tables covering the world in four volumes. The approach adopted for tidal prediction problems is considerably simplified in that an interpolation table based on a simple cosine curve is used. As mentioned previously, always use a standard layout when solving a tidal problem since a systematic approach reduces the chances of making an error. The following pages contain an extract from the Canadian Tide Tables.

STANDARD PORT **BHAVNAGAR** TIME ~~OR HEIGHT~~ REQUIRED **2100ZT**

SECONDARY PORT **SULTANPUR** DATE **16-8-79** TIME ZONE **−0530**

	TIME		HEIGHT	
	HW	LW	HW	LW
STANDARD PORT	1 **17~8~79 0019**	2 **16~8~79 1830**	3 **8·1**	4 **3·3**
Seasonal Changes in ML	− Standard Port		5 **NIL**	
	+ Secondary Port		6 **NIL**	
DIFFERENCES	7 **−0100**	8 **−0132**	9 **−2·9**	10 **−0·7**
SECONDARY PORT	11 **2319**	12 **1658**	13 **5·2**	14 **2·6**
DURATION	15 **0621**	RANGE(a)St (b)Sec	16(a) **4·8**	16(b) **2·6**

*Springs/Neaps/Interpolate

START –
Height at
Given Time ↓

REQUIRED TIME	17 **2100**
TIME HW	18 **2319**
INTERVAL	19 **0219**

FACTOR	20 **0·7**

RISE	21 **1·8**
HEIGHT LW	22 **2·6**
HEIGHT REQUIRED	23 **4·4**

↑
START –
Time for
Given Height

*Delete as necessary

Table of Height Differences from Nearest Predicted Level

Range	1	2	3	4	5	6	7	8	9	10
ft	ft	ft	ft	ft	ft	ft	ft	ft	ft	ft
1	.1	.1	.2	.2	.3	.3	.4	.4	.5	.5
2	.1	.2	.3	.4	.5	.6	.7	.8	.9	1.0
3	.2	.3	.5	.6	.8	.9	1.1	1.2	1.4	1.5
4	.2	.4	.6	.8	1.0	1.2	1.4	1.6	1.8	2.0
5	.3	.5	.8	1.0	1.3	1.5	1.8	2.0	2.3	2.5
6	.3	.6	.9	1.2	1.5	1.8	2.1	2.4	2.7	3.0
7	.4	.7	1.1	1.4	1.8	2.1	2.5	2.8	3.2	3.5
8	.4	.8	1.2	1.6	2.0	2.4	2.8	3.2	3.6	4.0
9	.5	.9	1.4	1.8	2.3	2.7	3.2	3.6	4.1	4.5
10	.5	1.0	1.5	2.0	2.5	3.0	3.5	4.0	4.5	5.0
11	.6	1.1	1.7	2.2	2.8	3.3	3.9	4.4	5.0	5.5
12	.6	1.2	1.8	2.4	3.0	3.6	4.2	4.8	5.4	6.0
13	.7	1.3	2.0	2.6	3.3	3.9	4.6	5.2	5.9	6.5
14	.7	1.4	2.1	2.8	3.5	4.2	4.9	5.6	6.3	7.0
15	.8	1.5	2.3	3.0	3.8	4.5	5.3	6.0	6.8	7.5
16	.8	1.6	2.4	3.2	4.0	4.8	5.6	6.4	7.2	8.0
17	.9	1.7	2.6	3.4	4.3	5.1	6.0	6.8	7.7	8.5
18	.9	1.8	2.7	3.6	4.5	5.4	6.3	7.2	8.1	9.0
19	1.0	1.9	2.9	3.8	4.8	5.7	6.7	7.6	8.6	9.5
20	1.0	2.0	3.0	4.0	5.0	6.0	7.0	8.0	9.0	10.0
21	1.1	2.1	3.2	4.2	5.3	6.3	7.4	8.4	9.5	10.5
22	1.1	2.2	3.3	4.4	5.5	6.6	7.7	8.8	9.9	11.0
23	1.2	2.3	3.5	4.6	5.8	6.9	8.1	9.2	10.4	11.5
24	1.2	2.4	3.6	4.8	6.0	7.2	8.4	9.6	10.8	12.0
25	1.3	2.5	3.8	5.0	6.3	7.5	8.8	10.0	11.3	12.5
26	1.3	2.6	3.9	5.2	6.5	7.8	9.1	10.4	11.7	13.0
27	1.4	2.7	4.1	5.4	6.8	8.1	9.5	10.8	12.2	13.5
28	1.4	2.8	4.2	5.6	7.0	8.4	9.8	11.2	12.6	14.0
29	1.5	2.9	4.4	5.8	7.3	8.7	10.2	11.6	13.1	14.5
30	1.5	3.0	4.5	6.0	7.5	9.0	10.5	12.0	13.5	15.0

Table of Time Intervals from Nearest Predicted Level

Duration	1	2	3	4	5	6	7	8	9
h m	h m	h m	h m	h m	h m	h m	h m	h m	h m
1 00	09	12	15	18	20	22	24	26	28
1 10	10	14	18	21	23	26	28	31	33
1 20	11	16	20	24	27	30	32	35	37
1 30	13	18	23	27	30	33	36	39	42
1 40	14	20	25	30	33	37	40	44	47
1 50	16	23	28	32	37	41	44	48	51
2 00	17	25	30	35	40	44	48	52	56
2 10	19	27	33	38	43	48	52	57	1 01
2 20	20	29	35	41	47	52	56	1 01	1 06
2 30	22	31	38	44	50	55	1 00	1 05	1 10
2 40	23	33	41	47	53	59	1 04	1 10	1 15
2 50	24	35	43	50	57	1 03	1 09	1 14	1 20
3 00	26	37	46	53	1 00	1 06	1 13	1 18	1 24
3 10	27	39	48	56	1 03	1 10	1 17	1 23	1 29
3 20	29	41	51	59	1 07	1 14	1 21	1 27	1 34
3 30	30	43	53	1 02	1 10	1 17	1 25	1 32	1 38
3 40	32	45	56	1 05	1 13	1 21	1 29	1 36	1 43
3 50	33	47	58	1 08	1 17	1 25	1 33	1 40	1 48
4 00	34	49	1 01	1 11	1 20	1 29	1 37	1 45	1 52
4 10	36	51	1 03	1 14	1 23	1 32	1 41	1 49	1 57
4 20	37	53	1 06	1 17	1 27	1 36	1 45	1 53	2 02
4 30	39	55	1 08	1 20	1 30	1 40	1 49	1 58	2 06
4 40	40	57	1 11	1 23	1 33	1 43	1 53	2 02	2 11
4 50	42	59	1 13	1 26	1 37	1 47	1 57	2 06	2 16
5 00	43	1 01	1 16	1 29	1 40	1 51	2 01	2 11	2 20
5 10	45	1 03	1 18	1 32	1 43	1 54	2 05	2 15	2 25
5 20	46	1 06	1 21	1 34	1 47	1 58	2 09	2 19	2 30
5 30	47	1 08	1 24	1 37	1 50	2 02	2 13	2 24	2 34
5 40	49	1 10	1 26	1 40	1 53	2 05	2 17	2 28	2 39
5 50	50	1 12	1 29	1 43	1 57	2 09	2 21	2 33	2 44
6 00	52	1 14	1 31	1 46	2 00	2 13	2 25	2 37	2 49
6 10	53	1 16	1 34	1 49	2 03	2 17	2 29	2 41	2 53
6 20	55	1 18	1 36	1 52	2 07	2 20	2 33	2 46	2 58
6 30	56	1 20	1 39	1 55	2 10	2 24	2 37	2 50	3 03
6 40	57	1 22	1 41	1 58	2 13	2 28	2 41	2 54	3 07
6 50	59	1 24	1 44	2 01	2 17	2 31	2 45	2 59	3 12
7 00	1 00	1 26	1 46	2 04	2 20	2 35	2 49	3 03	3 17
7 10	1 02	1 28	1 49	2 07	2 23	2 39	2 53	3 07	3 21
7 20	1 03	1 30	1 51	2 10	2 27	2 42	2 57	3 12	3 26
7 30	1 05	1 32	1 54	2 13	2 30	2 46	3 01	3 16	3 31
7 40	1 06	1 34	1 56	2 16	2 33	2 50	3 05	3 21	3 35
7 50	1 07	1 36	1 59	2 19	2 37	2 53	3 09	3 25	3 40
8 00	1 09	1 38	2 02	2 22	2 40	2 57	3 13	3 29	3 45
8 10	1 10	1 40	2 04	2 25	2 43	3 01	3 17	3 34	3 49
8 20	1 12	1 42	2 07	2 28	2 47	3 05	3 22	3 38	3 54
8 30	1 13	1 44	2 09	2 31	2 50	3 08	3 26	3 42	3 59
8 40	1 15	1 47	2 12	2 33	2 53	3 12	3 30	3 47	4 03
8 50	1 16	1 49	2 14	2 36	2 57	3 16	3 34	3 51	4 08
9 00	1 18	1 51	2 17	2 39	3 00	3 19	3 38	3 55	4 13
9 10	1 19	1 53	2 19	2 42	3 03	3 23	3 42	4 00	4 17
9 20	1 20	1 55	2 22	2 45	3 07	3 27	3 46	4 04	4 22
9 30	1 22	1 57	2 24	2 48	3 10	3 30	3 50	4 08	4 27
9 40	1 23	1 59	2 27	2 51	3 13	3 34	3 54	4 13	4 32
9 50	1 25	2 01	2 29	2 54	3 17	3 38	3 58	4 17	4 36
10 00	1 26	2 03	2 32	2 57	3 20	3 41	4 02	4 22	4 41
10 10	1 28	2 05	2 34	3 00	3 23	3 45	4 06	4 26	4 46
10 20	1 29	2 07	2 37	3 03	3 27	3 49	4 10	4 30	4 50
10 30	1 30	2 09	2 40	3 06	3 30	3 52	4 14	4 35	4 55
10 40	1 32	2 11	2 42	3 09	3 33	3 56	4 18	4 39	5 00
10 50	1 33	2 13	2 45	3 12	3 37	4 00	4 22	4 43	5 04
11 00	1 35	2 15	2 47	3 15	3 40	4 04	4 26	4 48	5 09
11 10	1 36	2 17	2 50	3 18	3 43	4 07	4 30	4 52	5 14
11 20	1 38	2 19	2 52	3 21	3 47	4 11	4 34	4 56	5 18
11 30	1 39	2 21	2 55	3 24	3 50	4 15	4 38	5 01	5 23
11 40	1 40	2 23	2 57	3 27	3 53	4 18	4 42	5 05	5 28
11 50	1 42	2 25	3 00	3 30	3 57	4 22	4 46	5 09	5 32
12 00	1 43	2 27	3 02	3 33	4 00	4 26	4 50	5 14	5 37

Interpolation

This is a general table for use with all ports and is based on the assumption that the tidal curve is a simple cosine curve. At most ports there is some distortion of the tidal curve. Where tides are small, therefore, interpolation is unnecessary when the calculated values of the duration, time interval, range and height difference do not coincide with those tabulated. Where the tides are large, however, interpolation is more desirable, but an estimate by eye is all that is justified by the ultimate accuracy of the prediction. When the duration or range of the tide are less than those tabulated in the calculation table, a direct arithmetic interpolation may be made.

SAINT JOHN (⁺⁴ HNA)

1979 MAY–MAI

Day	Time	Ht./ft.	Ht./m.	Jour	Heure	H./pi.	H./m.
1	0250	25.0	7.6	16	0215	26.6	8.2
TU	0910	4.3	1.3	WE	0835	2.2	.7
MA	1525	23.8	7.3	ME	1455	25.5	7.8
	2140	5.8	1.8		2100	3.9	1.2

TABLE 1

INFORMATION AND RANGE
RENSEIGNEMENTS ET AMPLITUDE

Reference port Port de référence	Index No. No. d'Index	Time zone Fuseau horaire	Position Latitude north Latitude nord	Position Longitude west Longitude ouest	Type of tide Genre de marées	Range/Amplitude Mean tide Marée moyenne	Range/Amplitude Large tide Grande marée
			° ′	° ′		ft./pi. m.	ft./pi. m
Tides/Marées Saint John	0 065	+4	45 16	66 04	SD	21.9 6.7	30.0 9.1

REFERENCE PORTS

TABLE 2

TIDAL HEIGHTS, EXTREMES AND MEAN WATER LEVEL
HAUTEURS DES MARÉES, EXTRÊMES ET NIVEAU MOYEN DE L'EAU

Reference port Port de référence	Heights / Hauteurs — Higher high water Pleine mer supérieures — Mean tide Marée moyenne	Large tide Grande marée	Lower low water Basse mer inférieures — Mean tide Marée moyenne	Large tide Grande marée	Recorded extremes Extrêmes enregistrés — Highest H.W. Extrême de pleine mer	Lowest L.W. Extrême de basse mer	Mean water level Niveau moyen de l'eau
	ft./pi. m.	ft./pi. m.	ft./pi. m.	ft./pi. m.	ft./pi. m.	ft./pi. m.	ft./pi. m.
Tides/Marées Saint John	25.3 7.7	29.6 9.0	3.4 1.0	−0.4 −0.1	29.6 9.0	−1.4 −0.4	14.5 4.4

SECONDARY PORTS

TABLE 3 Cont'd/Suite
INFORMATION AND TIDAL DIFFERENCES
RENSEIGNEMENTS ET DIFFÉRENCES DES MARÉES

Index no. *No. d'index*	Secondary port *Port secondaire*	Time zone *Fuseau horaire*	Position *Position* Lat. N. *Lat. N.*	Long. W. *Long. O.*	Differences *Différences* Higher high water *Pleine mer supérieure* Time *Heure*	Mean tide *Marée moyenne*	Large tide *Grande marée*	Lower low water *Basse mer inférieure* Time *Heure*	Mean tide *Marée moyenne*	Large tide *Grande marée*	Range *Amplitude* Mean tide *Marée moyenne*	Large tide *Grande marée*	Mean water level *Niveau moyen de l'eau*
			° ′	° ′	h. m.	ft./pi.	ft./pi.	h m	ft./pi.	ft./pi.	ft./pi.	ft./pi.	ft./pi.
	Area *Région* 1												
	Bay of Fundy North												
	Bay of Fundy Cont'd/Suite			on/*sur* SAINT JOHN, pages 2–5									
	Bay of Fundy North												
0129	St. Martins	+4	45 21	65 32	+0 06	+5.1	+6.3	+0 05	+0.8	−0.3	26.2	36.6	17.3
	Chignecto Bay North												
0140	Herring Cove	+4	45 34	64 58	+0 02	+8.2	+9.7	+0 09	+1.4	+0.4	28.7	39.0	19.1
0190	Cape Enrage	+4	45 36	64 47	+0 05	+10.4	+13.2	+0 22	+1.3	−0.1	31.0	43.3	20.3
	Shepody Bay												

Worked Example

Determine the predictions for the port of Saint John, New Brunswick on May 1st, 1979 and determine the height of the tide at 1800 zone time on the same day.

The predictions for the day in question are extracted directly from the tables as Saint John is a Standard or Reference Port.

The duration and range of the tide covering 1800 is then obtained.

The time interval from the nearest tide is required, in this case LW time is closest. Interval from nearest tide is 2h.35m.

The interpolation table on the right is entered with the duration (6h.15m.) and the column with the closest value to the interval is column 7.

Now moving to the interpolation table to the left and entering with the range (18.0) and column 7 gives the height difference as 6.3 feet.

This correction is applied to the height of the tide used in determining the interval, in this case HW.

SUGGESTED LAYOUT

REFERENCE PORT Saint John   TIME ZONE + 4   DATE 1/May/79

SECONDARY PORT   —   TIME ZONE   —

	REFERENCE PORT		SECONDARY PORT		
	Time	Height	Time	Height	
HW	0250	25.0	____	____	HW
LW	0910	4.3	____	____	LW
HW	1525	23.8	____	____	HW
LW	2140	5.8	____	____	LW

		Differences		
HHW/MT	____	____	____	HHW/MT
HHW/LT	____	____	____	HHW/LT
LLW/MT	____	____	____	LLW/MT
LLW/LT	____	____	____	LLW/LT

*REFERENCE/SECONDARY PORT (*Delete as required)

DURATION	0615
RANGE	18.0
*TIME FROM NEAREST TIDE	0235
*HEIGHT FROM NEAREST TIDE	____
*TIME/HEIGHT OF TIDE	23.8
*TIME/HEIGHT CORRECTION	−6.3
*TIME/HEIGHT PREDICTED	17.5 at 1800 on 1/May/79
CHARTED DEPTH	____
DEPTH OF WATER	____
DRAFT	____
DEPTH UNDER VESSEL	____